AF531356

ROLE OF WOMEN ENTREPRENEURSHIP IN SOCIAL DEVELOPMENT

ROLE OF WOMEN ENTREPRENEURSHIP IN SOCIAL DEVELOPMENT

Edited by
Dr. Suman Kalyan Chaudhury
M.Com., MBA, PGDPM & IR, LLB, Ph.D.
Reader cum Placement Officer
P.G. Department of Business Administration
Berhampur University
Berhampur
(Odisha)

DISCOVERY PUBLISHING HOUSE PVT. LTD.
NEW DELHI-110 002

Published by:
Tilak Wasan

DISCOVERY PUBLISHING HOUSE PVT. LTD.
4383/4B, Ansari Road, Darya Ganj
New Delhi-110 002 (India)
Phone : +91-11-23279245, 43596064-65
Fax : +91-11-23253475
E-mail : parul.wasan@gmail.com
discoverypublishinghouse@gmail.com
web : www.discoverypublishinggroup.com

***First Edition:* 2012**

ISBN: 978-93-5056-060-0

Role of Women Entrepreneurship in Social Development

Printed at:
Shree Balaji Art Press
Delhi

Preface

Women Entrepreneur is a person who accepts challenge to meet her personal needs and become economically independent by doing business. A strong desire to do something positive is an inbuilt quality of entrepreneurial women, who is capable of contributing values in both family and social life. In India, empowerment to women is not properly given, not only for involving into entrepreneurial activities, but also in day-to-day life. It is also going to give importance to the qualities of the women which are not fully identified by their self.

Regardless of the nature of enterprise, which may be on individual or group basis, the women enterer should have an organizational backing—an organization in which she is an equal partner along with other women and which can lend her support in terms of financial and non-financial services including credit, trading, business counselling, etc., besides being a forum for mutual support and collective action. It is appropriate to encourage women towards entrepreneurial activity with their 'empowerment' as the goal. The developmental professionals in their enthusiasm must not ignore the main subject, *i.e.*, the women themselves, for they already have definite function to perform in the family sphere.

The book offers empirical findings on various issues relating to entrepreneurship development among women. The book throws light to the fact that the problem of growing unemployment, regional imbalances, inequality in the distribution of income and wealth can be sorted out by providing training to the people of the country for self employment. It suggests various methods that may be followed to overcome various obstacles in the process of entrepreneurship development among women.

Dr. Suman Kalyan Chaudhury

Acknowledgements

Every action requires an initiator, influencer. I am initiated into writing this book, primarily, by the inspiration provided by my students and friends in the same profession. My colleagues are always stand with for support and cheering me. Therefore, I can't but gratefully acknowledge my indebtedness to all those who have extended generous assistance in the successful accomplishment of this indispensable work. It will be a serious blunder if I forget to mention some of my colleagues Prof. Niranjan Nayak, Center Head, Koustav Business School, Dr. Kirti Ranjan Swain, Associate Prof., IPSAR Business School, Cuttack, Dr. Ashok Kumar Panigrahi, Asst. Prof, RITEE Business School, Raipur, Prof. Ashok Kumar Panda, Dean, Astha school of management for their ardent encouragement and beacon guidance in bringing out this work.

I profusely thank my chairman of the institute, Er. Sundhansu Kumar Dash for his rock support and continuous push that furthered my efforts seamlessly towards quick accomplishment. My heartfelt gratitude to him.

Last but not least my heartfelt gratitude to my wife Sinu knows no bounds for her immaculate co-operation. Needless to depict, I am indebted to my family members for their love and affection and inspired me in my problem solving while in action.

I am also much beholden to Mr. Tilak Wasan, Managing Director, Discovery Publishing House Pvt. Ltd., New Delhi for publishing the work in a record time.

Dr. Suman Kalyan Chaudhury

Contents

List of Contributors

Dr. Sanjay R. Ajmeri, Lecturer in Commerce and Management, Bhikahbhai Jivabhai Vanijya Mahavidyalaya, Vallabh Vidyanagar, Anand (Gujarat).

Dr. Sushil Kumar Pattanaik, Senior Faculty in the Department of Commerce, KBDAV College, Nirakarpur, Khurda, (Odisha).

Dr. S.K. Das, Senior Faculty, Department of Commerce, PN (Auto) College, Khurda, (Odisha).

Dr. Veershetty Tadlapur, Asst. Prof, Department of Sociology, Government First Grade College, Kalgi–585 312, (Karnataka).

Dr. B.B. Padhiari, Reader, Department of Commerce, PN (Auto) College, Khurda, (Odisha).

Dr. D.S. Mohanty, Reader, Department of Commerce, PN (Auto) College, Khurda, (Odisha).

Dr. B.D. Behera, Reader, Department of Commerce, PN (Auto) College, Khurda, (Odisha).

Dr. Rais Ahmad, Department of Agricultural Economics and Business Management, AMU, Aligarh, (U.P.)

Mr. Ashraf Imam, Ex-Branch Manager-Reliance Life Insurance-Sikandrarao Branch-Aligarh Region and Currently Enrolled as PhD Student—Department of Commerce-Aligarh Muslim University, Aligarh, (U.P.)

Prof. Aparajita Biswal, Lecturer, A and A Economics, Utkal University, Bhubaneswar, (Odisha).

Prof. Sanjay Kanti Das, Assistant Professor, Commerce, Lumding College, Lumding, Nagaon, (Assam).

Dr. Veershetty G Rathod, Assistant Professor, Department of Commerce and Management, Sahyadri Arts and Commerce College, Kuvempu University, Shimoga – 577 203, (Karnataka).

Dr. Prafulla Chandra Mahapatra, Principal, Rajsunakhala College, Rajsunakhala, Nayagarh, (Odisha).

Mr. Jaba Varadwaj, Research Scholar, M.F.C. (Utkal), Utkal University, Bhubaneswar, (Odisha).

The Women Entrepreneurship *The Generation Next*

Dr. Veershetty Tadlapur

ABSTRACT

Women Entrepreneurs may be defined as the women or a group of women who initiate, organize and operate a business enterprise. Government of India has defined women entrepreneurs as an enterprise owned and controlled by a woman having a minimum financial interest of 51 per cent of the capital and giving at least 51 per cent of employment generated in the enterprise to women. Like a male entrepreneurs a women entrepreneur has many functions. They should explore the prospects of starting new enterprise; undertake risks, introduction of new innovations, coordination administration and control of business and providing effective leadership in all aspects of business. Acceptance of women entrepreneurs is a fact today. Twenty years ago a woman entrepreneur was looked at with hesitation and non-belief. It took a considerable effort to establish her bonafide and it had to be proved that she meant business. The entry of women in organized business is a fairly recent phenomenon. The entrepreneurial style adopted by women was different from that of men. Studies have revealed that women focus more on intuition and relationships for running business, while men emphasize logic and efficiency. What cockles one's heart is that more and more women are taking risks only to see a better tomorrow.

Introduction

The Indian economy has been witnessing a drastic change since mid -1991, with new policies of economic liberalization, globalization and privatization initiated by the Indian Government. India has great entrepreneurial potential. At present, women involvement in economic activities is marked by a low work participation rate, excessive concentration in the unorganized sector and employment in less skilled jobs. Any strategy aimed at economic development will be lop-sided without involving women who constitute half of the world's population. Evidence has unequivocally established that entrepreneurial spirit is not a male prerogative. Women entrepreneurship has gained momentum in the last three decades with the increase in the number of women enterprises and their substantive contribution to economic growth. The industrial performance of Asia-Pacific region propelled by Foreign Direct Investment, technological innovations and manufactured exports has brought a wide range of economic and social opportunities to women entrepreneurs.

In this dynamic world, women entrepreneurs are an important part of the global quest for sustained economic development and social progress. In India, though women have played a key role in the society, their entrepreneurial ability has not been properly tapped due to the lower status of women in the society. It is only from the Fifth Five Year Plan (1974-78) onwards that their role has been explicitly recognized with a marked shift in the approach from women welfare to women development and empowerment. The development of women entrepreneurship has become an important aspect of our plan priorities. Several policies and programmes are being implemented for the development of women entrepreneurship in India.

There is a need for changing the mindset towards women so as to give equal rights as enshrined in the constitution. The progress towards gender equality is slow and is partly due to the failure to attach money to policy commitments. In the words of president APJ Abdul Kalam "empowering women is a prerequisite for creating a good nation, when women are empowered, society with stability is assured. Empowerment of women is essential as their thoughts and their value systems lead to the development of a good family, good society and ultimately a good nation." When a woman is empowered it does not mean that another individual becomes powerless or is having less power. On the contrary, if a women is empowered her competencies towards decision-making will surely influence her family's behavior. In advanced countries, there is a phenomenon of increase in the number of self-employed women after the world war 11. In USA, women own 25 per cent of all business, even though their sales on an average are less than two-fifths of those of other small business. In Canada, women own one-third of small business and in France it is one-fifth.

"Entrepreneur is an Innovative Agent Who Introduces Something New into the Economy—A New Method of Production, A New Source of Material or New Markets"

An entrepreneur's function is to revolutionize the pattern of production by exploiting an invention or introducing an untried technological; possibility for producing a new commodity.

David McCleland, who attributed entrepreneurial aspirations to personality traits, states that people with high need achievement, work harder, learn faster, do better work than others of the same IQ, they also seem to do their best when it speaks of their credentials and not about special incentives offered to perform well. They are more resistant to social pressure, choose experts rather than friends as their partners in their work activities and have a liking for risky occupations.

"The Spirit of Desire for Individual Achievement is the Basis of Entrepreneurship"

The development of a society depends more on the attitude of people than on the scarcity of factors of production. Since attitude cannot be influenced, it is possible to change the attitude and develop the cult of entrepreneurship as the prime mover of economic development.

Empirical works substantiating this partial picture of 'Self-made' entrepreneur have also appeared in developed and developing countries. During the late sixties small-sectors began to be recognized as instrumental for tapping latent entrepreneurial talent. In the initial stages government envisaged a promotional package to setup units. The package consisted of financial assistance, incentives, infrastructural facilities, technical and managerial guidance through a network of a number of support organizations at Central, State and local levels.

Entrepreneurial growth requires focus on the human resource development more than anything else. Since then, the entrepreneurship development programmes have became an integral part of our economic development programme.

The objectives of these EDPs could be broadly put as follows:

- Increasing the number of entrepreneurs who start new business units;
- Diversifying the social base of entrepreneurs from non-conventional sources;
- Improving the quality of entrepreneurship to reduce the incidence of industrial sickness;
- Reducing the incidence of unemployment by creating opportunities for self-employment.

The above objectives are attempted to be achieved through a well-designed EDP, which include three important stages like:

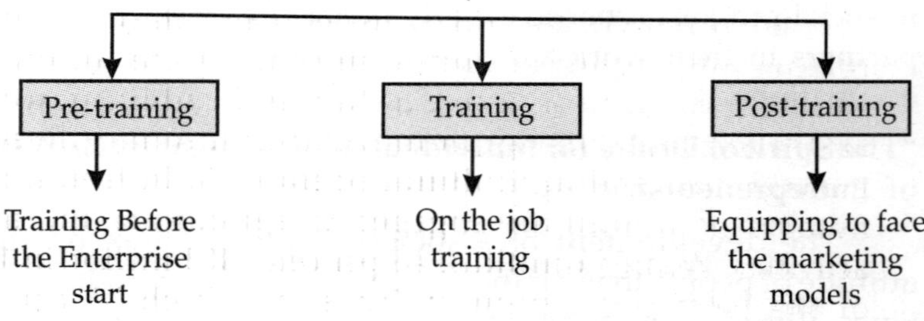

The aspirants for entrepreneurial training are selected on the basis of certain psychological variables like:

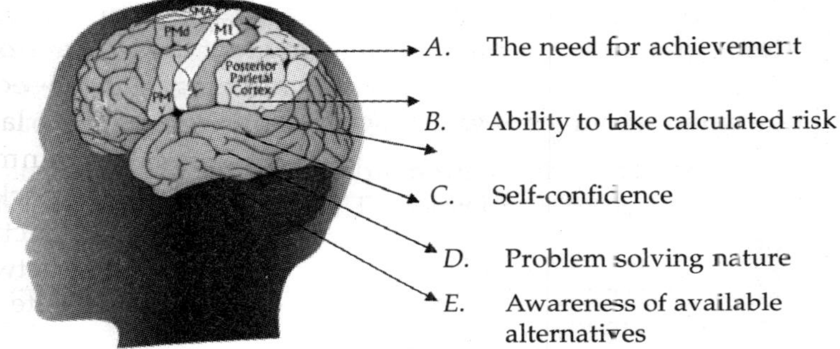

Entrepreneurial aspirants have to change their mind set by acquiring new ideas and skills during the training period consciously and consistently.

McClelland in his book 'The Achieving Society' observes that growth of an economy depends on the achievement motivation of its inhabitants. Any development programme has to take note of the socio-cultural special facilities of different societies. In case of an economy like ours, the active government participation in the development process is to be considered. Thus the development programmes in general and Entrepreneur Development programme in particular have to accommodate the notion of plurality in approach to development. Because, "A good entrepreneur is one who is capable of inspiring confidence in people and has the ability to motivate them to work with him in fulfilling the economic goals set by him".

From time immemorial women have played a pivotal role in building better homes, in shaping the society and sowing seeds for a prosperous Nation. In addition, women also have contributed significantly in income earning, livestock management and agricultural operations. In fact, a large number of women are engaged in agriculture and allied activities. Women constitute 48 per cent (403 million in 1991) of the total population in India, of which 23 per cent

(91 million) of women are engaged in agriculture and allied activities, household industries, and service sectors.

The economic status of women is now accepted as an indicator of a society's stage of development. It is therefore, in the interest of a society to make full and most effective use of its human resources of which women form an integral part.

Women are doing commendable work. These women are called micro-entrepreneurs. They do it because of two reasons, *viz*:

1. To earn more income and also to overcome the problems of middlemen;
2. To attain socio-economic empowerment;

Empowerment of Women through the Following Strategies:

1. Educating girls and women;
2. Facilitating their involvement in economic activities through development of their entrepreneurial and income earning capabilities and access to credit;
3. Involving women in policy formulation and decision-making;
4. Encouraging socio-cultural change by exploring gender issues and promoting effective implementation of equal rights through legislation.

The word '*Entrepreneur*' appeared in the French language long before the emergence of the concept of the entrepreneurial function. In 18th century the word was used to refer to economic activity. Arthur.H.Cole; defines entrepreneurship as "The purposeful activity (including an integrated sequence of decisions) of an individual or a group of associated individuals undertaking to initiate, maintain or aggrandize a profit oriented business unit for the production or distribution of economic goods and services".

Woman entrepreneurs are the women or a group of woman who initiate, organize and operate a business enterprise. The Government of India connotes women entrepreneurs as "An enterprise owned and controlled by women having a minimum financial interest of 51 per cent of the capital and giving at least 51 per cent of the employment generated in the enterprise to women".

Indian women of today have taken many strides towards business ownership. The broad classification of women business owners include women who establish, inherit, or acquire a business; women who start businesses with spouses or business partners but are either at the forefront or behind the scenes; and finally, women who start fast-growing or part-time or slow-growing firms. Although earlier researches on women entrepreneurs have suggested that significant differences existed between female and male entrepreneurs. However, more recent studies have shown that there are far more similarities than differences between women and men entrepreneurs in terms of psychological and demographic characteristics. The dominant predictors of success in case of women entrepreneurs are work experience and years of self-employment.

Generally, women view their businesses as a cooperative network of relationships rather than as a distinct profit-generating entity. This network extends beyond the business into the entrepreneur's relationships with her family and the community. Certain cross-cultural studies on women entrepreneurs have reported that their management styles emphasizes open communication and participative decision-making, and their business goals reflect a concern for the community in which the business operates. The majority of women business owners operate enterprises in the service sectors, whereas the majority of male business owners operate enterprises in non service sectors, particularly manufacturing. Women are not only achieving economic independence and wealth creation for themselves, but through job creation, they are also providing opportunities for others, particularly for other women. A series of researches have shown that the workforce of women-owned businesses tend to be more gender balanced than the workforce of men-owned businesses, although women business owners are more likely to hire women. Put simply, an investment in women's entrepreneurship is an investment in the economic independence and well-being of all women.

The Characteristics of Women Entrepreneurs in India

In comparison to their women counterparts who established their businesses two decades earlier, women who have started their businesses sometime during the past decade are more likely to have the following:

- a higher level of education, previous professional and managerial experience, as well as executive level experience;
- a greater appetitive for capital, both credit and equity;
- a strong motivation for autonomy and achievement;
- a dynamic personality;
- a passion for what they do;
- creativity to innovate and implement;
- independence and self reliance;
- high self confidence;
- willingness and ability to take risks;
- alertness to oppurtinities;
- ability to marshal resources;
- ability to respond to market and environment signals.

Types of Women Entrepreneurs

- **Natural Entrepreneurs**

Those who take business as a profession on their own either by self pre-planning or motivated through profit/ money factor and also for keeping themselves busy.

- **Created Entrepreneurs**

Those who have been encouraged and trained through specialized training programmes such as Entrepreneurship Development programmes to set up independent business.

- **Forced Entrepreneurs**

Those who are compelled by circumstances such as the death of father or husband with responsibilities falling on them-to take over existing business.

- **The Bename Entrepreneurs**

Those who are acting as a façade for business of their husband or brother.

The list of successful women entrepreneurs is quite long who have excelled not only in India only but have thrived abroad. Shanaz Husain (pioneered and popularized the Indian herbal heritage world-wide), Deepika Seth Dhar, Yashodhara Shoroff, Geetha Anand, Sumita Morarji, Simonne Tata, Kiran Muziumdar are few names who have made a mark in their respective areas of activities in the country.

This type of achievement on the part of women entrepreneur provides a pointer to the huge developmental potential that could be harnessed if properly handled and helped. This class of entrepreneurs is endowed with high drive, creativity and innovation for taking on the challenging role of entrepreneurship. The SWOT analysis of women entrepreneurs (Rani, 1996) revealed that the strengths and opportunities were higher in degree than weaknesses and threats. Commitment and complete dedication to their enterprise were found to be major strength of women entrepreneurs followed by systematic approach and family support.

Today several associations of women entrepreneurs are operating at National level and International level.

At International level there are two Associations *viz.*:

(a) Associated Country Women of the World (ACWW) with 30 million women entrepreneurs as its members.

(b) World Association of Women Entrepreneurs (WAWE) which also to collaborate with Indian women for joint ventures.

At the National Level, the following Institutions are Widely Known

(a) Woman Entrepreneurs wing of National Alliance of Young Entrepreneurs (NAYE).

(b) Association of Women Entrepreneurs of Karnataka (AWEK).

(c) Indian council of Women Entrepreneurs, New Delhi.

(d) Self-Employed Women's Association (SEWA).

The Objectives of these Associations are:

(i) To provide a meeting ground

(ii) To present the problems to the concerned authorities

(iii) To encourage Managerial Development Programmes to solve the problems of Women Entrepreneurs.

Problems are faced by Women Enterpreneurs in India

1. Women hardly interact with other women who are successful entrepreneurs. This results in a negative impact on their networking skills.
2. The areas, where one can see women acting as entrepreneurs, is in the very typical women's sectors of 3Ps. This is also the area, where women are accepted in society to be experts in and thus have the capacity for entrepreneurial activities.
3. It is clear, that women have the responsibility of getting children and taking care of them. Very few societies accept fathers taking over the role of staying home and taking care of the children. Once these children are old enough to take care for themselves, they have to bear an additional responsibility of taking care of elder parents. If they want to become entrepreneurs, the society expects them to be able to do both: take care of family and home and do business.

4. Women are very critical when it comes to themselves – can I really do this, am I good enough, maybe I have to learn more, others can do it better. It is quite interesting that many successful women have been educated in only girls colleges and schools, which often deliver a safe environment to try out ones personal strengths, learn to overcome weaknesses and be proud of oneself.

5. *Discrimination:* It is hard to believe but women are still treated differently in our society. Women do get lower salaries compared to men doing the same job, women do not have access to men dominated networks who take their decisions about successors in the company during golf plays or sauna meetings....

6. *Missing networks:* Through centuries business men have build up their networks but women still have to learn to catch up.

7. A lot of women tell stories about not being taken serious by bankers, when they wanted to get a loan for their business. Often enough, they have to bring their husbands or fathers to be able to be heard and receive financing. So, the domination of men in the banking world is a problem.

Suggestions for Development of Women Entrepreneurship

1. The first and foremost suggestion in my view is that of conducting of entrepreneurial awareness camps to make them aware of their hidden entrepreneurial capabilities and motivate them to do justice to their capabilities.

2. In order to motivate new women entrepreneurs, case studies and audio visuals of successful women entrepreneurs should be prepared. These stories of several women entrepreneurs will improve the environment for women. It is in this context that collaborative associations of urban and rural women entrepreneurs are formed.

3. Banks should not only serve as lending institutions but also play the role of a promoter. Special training-cum-orientation programmes for appraising of bank officers and agencies should be planned to change their biased attitudes towards the women entrepreneurs.
4. There should be separate allocation of funds by the centre exclusively for the development of women entrepreneurs.

Conclusion

Women entrepreneurship development is an essential part of human resource development. The development of women entrepreneurship is very low in India, especially in the rural areas. Entrepreneurship amongst women has been a recent concern. Women have become aware of their existence their rights and their work situation. However, women of middle class are not too eager to alter their role in fear of social backlash. The progress is more visible among upper class families in urban cities. It may be said that the Women Entrepreneurs who are emerging as a force nowadays associate through networking which must be encouraged and supported both by government and family. It must be realised that the women who constitute half of the population must be brought to the main stream by means of entrepreneurial activities so that they can effectively contribute productively to the women community in particular through empowerment and overall economic development of the country in general.

References

1. Desai, Aravind Rai N.- "Environment and Entrepreneur ", Ashish Publishing House, New Delhi, 1989
2. Peter. F. Drucker-"Innovations and Entrepreneurship", East-West Press Pvt. Ltd., N D, 1991, p. 19.
3. Anitha.H.S.- "Entrepreneurship Development—Role of Commercial Bank", MDP Jaipur 2003.
4. *Southern Economist*— "Women Entrepreneurship in India"—By H.S. Anitha And A.S. Laxmisha

5. *Southern Economist* — "Micro Women Entrepreneurs and Socio-economic Empowerment: — A Study" — By L. Rathakrishnan and B. Sellammalle.

6. *Southern Economist*—"Women Entrepreneurs in India:— Scope and Opportunities"—By Shreegouri V Savadi.

7. *Southern Economist* — "Emerging Profile of Women Entrepreneurs and Workers in India" — By L.N.Dahiya.

8. *Southern Economist*— "Global Women Entrepreneurs Profile:—An Analysis" — By N.Manimekalai and R.Ganesan.

9. *Southern Economist* —"Entrepreneurship Development Programmes:— An Analysis" — By Udaya kumar and T.N. Sreedhara.

Management of Tourism Entrepreneurship

Dr. B.B. Padhiari, Dr. B.D. Behera,
Mr. D.S. Mohanty

'India lives in villages'. This adage emphasizes rural character of Indian demography to which great attention was given by the Father of the Nation, who evoked 'If the villages perish India will perish too'.

ABSTRACT

Land both private and public is the main source of livelihood in rural areas, with agriculture, animal husbandry, forestry and allied activities. While India is emerging as one of the fastest growing economies witnessing a steady GDP growth of around 9 per cent. However, the pace of growth is not homogenous throughout the country. Rural India is unable to match the speed of development and growth of urban India. In India where the large majority of population live in rural areas (about 70 %), rural entrepreneurship should be recognized as the basis of rural development since it is considered as the essential link in the overall socio-economic development, employment generation and poverty alleviation in rural areas. Entrepreneurship is a process where a person is self employed and also provides job for others and is called as an entrepreneur. Hence, entrepreneurship is characterized by self employment which contributes a lot towards the national income of a country and leads to achieve a balanced economic growth.

However, limited availability of land as well as unequal distribution of land among the rural population create a serious problem for full time employment opportunities of rural people. Hence, most of the rural agriculturist and farming entrepreneurs are remaining under Below Poverty Line (BPL) in spite of their hard work throughout the year. Besides, rural industrialization has not taken off very far despite adequate attention given to it by the Government as well as by the planners since independence. Therefore, it is the need of the hour to create additional employment opportunities in rural areas. Tourism entrepreneurship of various vocations in rural areas may be considered as one of the right solutions to such an acute problem.

The present study is designed to cover various vocations present in the tourist centres of coastal Odisha. The study includes both tropical as well as common vocations found in different tourist places. More specifically three coastal districts of Odisha namely, Puri, Cuttack, and Khurda are taken for the purpose of study as tourists in large number, domestic and international visit these districts in most parts of the year.

The methodology adopted in the study was of both empirical as well as analytical with the reference period of two years i,.e., 2007 – 08 and 2008 – 09. The second part of the study has explained the method of data collection, the third part has expressed the method of data processing while the last part has covered the factors responsible for decline of the vocation and conclusion.

Keywords: Adage, demography, evoked, perish, livelihood, allied activities, emerging, witnessing, poverty alleviation, vocation, potential, methodology, empirical, analytical, respondent, occupants, vendors, exhibit, attributed, survey, outweigh, prominent, incidentally, contrast, pattern, probably, seemingly, turnover, minority, at par, secure, fetch, negligible, corresponding, strikingly, Noteworthy, significant, affirmative, inheritance, unbiased, contradictory, pessimism, corroborated, slide, narrowed down, detrimental, underscore, outstripping, baffling, multidimensional.

Introduction

Land both private and public is the main source of livelihood in rural areas, with agriculture, animal husbandry, forestry and allied activities. While India is emerging as one of the fastest growing economies witnessing a steady GDP growth of around 9 per cent. However, the pace of growth is not homogenous throughout the country. Rural India is unable to match the speed of development and growth of urban India. In India where the large majority of population live in rural areas (about 70%), rural entrepreneurship should be recognized as the basis of rural development since it is considered as the essential link in the overall socio-economic development, employment generation and poverty alleviation in rural areas. Entrepreneurship is a process where a person is self employed and also provides job for others and is called as an entrepreneur. Hence, entrepreneurship is characterized by self employment which contributes a lot towards the national income of a country and leads to achieve a balanced economic growth.

However, limited availability of land as well as unequal distribution of land among the rural population create a serious problem for full time employment opportunities of rural people. Hence, most of the rural agriculturist and farming entrepreneurs are remaining under Below Poverty Line (BPL) in spite of their hard work throughout the year. Besides, rural industrialization has not taken off very far despite adequate attention given to it by the Government. as well as by the planners since independence. Hence it is badly required to create additional employment opportunities in rural areas. Tourism entrepreneurship of various vocations in rural areas may be considered as one of the right solutions to such an acute problem.

Ever since Independence, the Standard of Living in the State has been below the national average. In 1950-51, Odisha's real per capita income was about 90 per cent of the national average. However, the States, real per capita income had begun to slide thereafter and come down to about 61 per cent of the national average in 2002-03. This long-term falling trend in real per capita income since 2004-05 has not only been arrested, but reversed as well. It is observed that the

State's per capita income has started rising and the gap with the average national per capita income has been reducing steadily w.e.f. the year 2004-05. So far as the real growth rates of the state during the first decade of the current century is concerned, it is again observed that the growth rate of the State exceeded the national growth rate in five out of nine years. However, in the last year, the excess of the State's growth rate over the national rate narrowed down. Hence, it is the need of the hour, to put in extra effort so that Odisha's economy continues to grow much faster and higher than the national average to catch up fast with the rest of India.

In this chapter an attempt has been made to highlight the management of rural tourism entrepreneurship with special reference to socio-economic status of various tourism vocational entrepreneurs in three coastal districts of Odisha.

Vocations and Tourist Places

Tourism Vocation in Odisha may be grouped under different categories at Tourist places of three coastal districts namely Puri, Cuttack, and Khurda basing on varying nature of jobs and services rendered by tourism entrepreneurs . Tourism vocation at various tourist centres may have different occupation as per the need and requirement of tourists of the country and abroad. Tourist centres may be rural or urban tourist centres. But most the tourist entrepreneurs are the permanent resident of nearby villages. The villagers who have neither substantial landed property, nor sound enough in finance may prefer tourism vocation as their self employment opportunities with very low financial investment. The following Table 2.1 presents various tourism vocations at different tourist places in three coastal districts of Odisha. The table reflects twenty nos. of tourism entrepreneurs who are separately identified by rendering their own vocational activities to earn their day to day livelihood.

Table 2.1: Vocations and Tourist Places

Sl. No.	Vocations	Tourist Places
1.	Priest	Jagannath Temple, Mangala Temple, Alarnath, Barunei, Gouri Temple, Lokanath temple Gundicha Mandir, Ramachandi, Sun Temple, Sakhigopal, Lingaraj Temple, Dhableswar, Charchika, Bhatarika, Bhagabati , Narayani
2.	Bhog, Dhup, Prasad and flower	-do-
3.	Shoe stand	-do-
4.	Tourist Guide	Puri, Konark, Lingaraj Temple
5.	Handicraft	Puri, Cuttack , Konark
6.	Stone works	Puri , Konark
7.	Wood work	Puri , Konark, Bhubaneswar, Raghurajpur
8.	Patta painting	Raghurajpur, Puri
9.	Home works	Konark, Puri, Cuttack
10.	Filigree	Cuttack
11.	Appliqué work	Pipli
12.	Photography	Puri, Konark, Bhubaneswar, Satapada, Chilika
13.	Swimming, facilitator	Puri, Chandrabhaga
14.	Boatman	Chilika, Satapada, Dhabaleswar
15.	Restaurants	Puri, Konark, Bhubaneswar, Cuttack, Banpur, Kakatapur, Sakhigopal, Pipli, Balugaon
16.	Stationary shop	All places except Ramachandi, Narayani and Raghurajpur
17.	Juice-vendor Tea stall	All places
18.	PCO	All places excluding Narayani and Dhabaleswar
19.	Bettle shop	All places
20.	Horse & camel rider	Puri sea beach

The handicraft entrepreneurs may further be categorized into stone work, wood work, patta paintings, horn works, filigree and appliqué work. All these vocations are professionally practised at various tourist places as mentioned in the table.

Relatively smaller vocations are photography, swimming facilitator, boatman etc. photography is mainly observed at Konark, Puri, Satapada and Chilika. Swimming facilitators are specifically seen in sea beaches of Puri and Chandrabhaga. Boatman is a major vocation at Satapada and Chilika lake lagoon as most of the tourists avail boating services.

There are shops like stationeries, restaurants, PCOs, bettle shops, juice-vendors and mobile vendors who also operate their tourism entrepreneurial activities at various tourist centres. In addition to the above vocations, horse and camel riding have been found to be popular attractions only at Puri sea beach. In view of its popularity it is also included in the list of tourism vocations. For the purpose of analysis, tourist centres are identified in three coastal districts of Odisha along with specific places of tourist spots on the basis of their historical, religious and cultural importance. It is observed that more tourist spots are located in Khurda and Puri district. More tourists spots of Cuttack and Puri districts are outside the towns while few spots are found outside the city in Khurda district.

Age Group of the Respondents

All the vocational occupants under study are classified under four age groups. Age group is an important determinant of one's decision regarding the vocation or profession he/ she opts for. While persons in the higher age group are not likely to leave their vocation, younger persons have the possibility of switching over to other vocations or professions. Among other variables, 'age' has significant bearing on this decision. The four age groups are as between 15-25, 25-35, 35-45 and 45 and above,. Table 2.2 depicts the age group of different occupants.

While Examining age group of respondents in various occupation categories, it is observed that most people are in the age group of 25-35. It constitutes nearly a third of total occupants or one-third of the whole sample. It is followed by the age group of 45 and above where 23.8 per cent of the total occupants fall. Priests comprise the major group. *i.e.,* 25 per cent of the vocational occupants. In this group the majority fall in the age group 25-35, followed by the age group of 45 and above. Priests are mostly villagers and it is a family tradition to serve in the temples. Those members of the traditional Sevayat families who have not found employment opportunity elsewhere on the temple service. After the age of 25, they find little scope for other opportunities and accept priesthood as the permanent vocation. It is seen that the children of these priests who also assist their parents in this vocation fall in the age group of 15-25 while seeking opportunities elsewhere. This can be attributed to the lowest percentage, *i.e.,* 7.7 per cent of the total number of priests.

Puja material vendors in maximum number fall in the age group of 35-45 followed by that of 25-35. However, the age group of 15-25 is found to be significant in contrast to other occupations. It implies that persons invariably in all age groups are engaged as puja material vendors. There is no marked difference in the number between different age groups. As a practice, this is also considered as a family tradition, where occupants themselves prefer their children to be employed. Most of them seem to have chosen the vocation by compulsion or family requirement or family tradition.

The age group pattern of shoe stand owners demonstrates a different picture while the age group of 15-25 seems to be dominant. It constitutes 40 per cent of the total sample. The percentage difference between other age groups is small. This indicates that the relatively young persons are engaged in the vocation. Through discussion with these occupants, it is revealed that most of them the in vocation initially and as they grow in age, they switch to other vocations at the tourist centers or elsewhere. Moreover, Photography as a vocation has attracted persons from all age groups whereas that of 35-45 is found to be dominating with 32 per cent of them in this age. The two other age groups, which include 25-35 and 45 and above employ same percentage of photographers that is about a fourth. This clearly demonstrates that photographers at the tourist places are evenly distributed so far as the group is concerned.

Table 2.2: Respondents Age Groups

Sl. No	Vocations	Years									
		15–25		25–35		35–45		45 & above		Total No	
		1	%	2	%	3	%	4	%	5	%
1.	Priest	12	7.7	61	39.1	34	21.8	49	31.4	156	100
2.	Pooja material vendors	14	25.4	18	32.7	16	29.0	07	12.9	55	100
3.	Shoe stand	06	40.0	03	20.0	04	26.7	02	13.3	15	100
4.	Photography	05	20.0	06	24.0	08	32.0	06	24.0	25	100
5.	Guide	01	5.0	10	50	04	20.0	05	25.0	20	100
6.	Drinks	15	33.3	16	35.6	09	20.0	05	11.1	45	100
7.	Nolia	01	6.67	05	33.33	07	46.7	02	13.3	15	100
8.	Boatman	03	14.3	10	47.6	06	28.6	02	09.52	21	100
9.	Restaurant	14	31.8	14	31.8	05	11.4	11	25.0	44	100
10.	Stationaryshop	20	38.46	61	39.1	34	21.8	49	31.4	156	100
11.	Peddlers	12	28.6	10	23.8	07	16.7	13	30.9	42	100
12.	Bettle shop	11	25.6	09	20.45	09	20.45	15	34.1	44	100
13.	Handicraft	07	11.3	25	40.3	12	19.3	18	29.03	62	100
14.	PCOs	06	27.3	08	36.3	06	27.3	02	9.1	22	100
15.	Entertainment with Horse etc	01	8.33	04	33.33	05	41.7	02	16.7	12	100
16	**Total**	**128**	**20.3**	**21**	**33.6**	**14**	**22.8**	**14.8**	**23.3**	**630**	**100**

Source: Primary Data Collected.

Analysis of the age group of guides reveal a clear picture. Most of the guides employed, *i.e.*, 50 per cent of the total sample are found in the age group of 25-35. As a matter of fact, they require basic education about places of tourist importance. In order to perform their function as guides. they also need to communicate in 2-3 languages. This is perhaps the major reasons for which they are mostly in the group of 25-35. Similarly guides do not fall under the age group of 15-25 mainly due to the fact that they do not acquire the required skill for the vocation at that age. Guides are also found seldom in the sample from other age groups.

Drink vendors which include green coconut, juice vendors, are seen mostly in the age group of 15-25 and 25-35. Relatively elder persons are not engaged in this vocation. Analyzing the age group of Nolias who function at different. sea beaches, a majority of them fall in the age group 25-35 and 35-45. They need swimming skill while it is a vocation requiring sound health and physique. This is the reason behind the fact that middle-aged persons dominate in this category. Among the restaurant owners near tourist places, the popular age group appears to be 45 and above, followed by 15-35. It seems that they scattered across all age groups while nothing clear emerges from their age analysis. With regard to stationary shop owners, the predominant age group is 15-25, followed by 35-45, The distribution of these occupants in other two groups is almost equal. Moreover, similar trend is observed when we examine the distribution of age group of peddlers and bettle shop owners. No specific age group is found to have noticeable presence.

However, among the occupants dealing in handicrafts, the majority falls in the age group of 25-35. This is considered reasonable due to the skill required for the vocation. While no specific age group is found to be dominating among the PCO owners, the age group of 25- 35 is found to be significant among entertainers. These persons use camels and horses for entertaining the visitors at the tourist places. Children find their entertainment most attractive and tourist families prefer middle aged persons to perform these entertainments in view of the safety of their children. On the overall analysis, it can be inferred that the vocations that require specific skill and knowledge mostly employ middle-aged persons. In case of other vocations, the distribution of occupants' age is almost even exceptionally rare.

Earning Members and their Dependants

The vocational occupants are mostly local people coming from nearby villages. In city areas also majority of them are from nearby places. It is observed that most of them practice the vocation as a hereditary business. Table 2.3 signifies about the earning members of the Vocational occupants and their dependants.

Table 2.3: Earning Members and Their Dependants

Vocation	Earning members				Dependants			
	One		Two		1-3		3-5	
	No	%	No	%	No	%	No	%
Priest	120	76.9	36	23.1	96	61.5	60	39.5
Poojamaterial vendors	45	81.8	10	19.2	32	58.18	23	41.82
Shoe stand	9	60	6	40	10	66.66	5	33.34
Photography	16	64	9	36	15	60	10	40
Guide	12	60	8	40	12	60	8	60
Drinks	32	58.18	13	41.82	26	57.7	19	42.3
Nolia	9	60	6	40	7	46.6	8	63.4
Boatman	14	66.6	7	33.4	11	52.4	10	47.6
Restaurant	25	56.8	19	43.2	30	68.2	14	31.8
Stationary	32	61.5	20	38.5	25	38	27	52
Bettle shop	30	71.4	12	28.6	25	59.5	17	40.5
Handicraft	42	62.7	20	32.3	32	51.6	30	48.4
PCOs	15	68.2	7	31.8	12	54.5	10	45.5
Entertainers	8	66.6	4	33.4	5	41.6	7	58.4
Total	**409**	**64.9**	**221**	**35.1**	**338**	**53.7**	**292**	**46.33**

Source; Primary Data Collected

While discussion with various vocational occupants they reply that the number of earning members of the family is either one or two. We have classified the same earning members of the respondents' family accordingly. Generally, majority of them (65%) have one earning member per family whereas, the rest have two. This trend is found across all vocational groups.

Nearly 3/4th among the largest group, *i.e.*, priests and Puja material vendors replied to have one earning member in their family. However, they seem to have bias in their opinion. Further, in other vocations, the distribution of respondents shows 65 per cent in one earning member category while 35 per cent in two earning member category. This distribution is found to be similar to the general trend.

The respondents were also asked to state the number of dependents in the family. On the basis of their response, the number of dependents was classified into two groups, *i.e.*, 1-3 and 3-5. The average number of respondents in the first category is 53.7 and the rest is found to be 46.3 in the second category. While classifying all respondents in to vocation categories, we observe a significant trend. In the large groups of vocations, *i.e.*, priests, Puja material vendors and shoe stand owners; the number of dependents is mostly 1-3 while 65 per cent of the respondents in these categories opined that they have 1-3 dependents. In other categories, however, respondents were evenly distributed with regard to the number of dependents. At the same time, the trend seems to be reasonable along expected lines considering the rural and village base of the respondents.

Qualification

Table 2.4 exhibits the educational qualifications of different types of the occupants. Though qualifications greatly vary from vocation to vocation and within the same vocation, great majority, *i.e*, 74 per cent among the priests are found to have graduate qualification and above. Whereas a little of only 10 per cent among the restaurant owners and guides are found to be under matriculates. About 64 per cent among the restaurant owners are graduates or more while only 14 per cent of them are under matriculates. This may be due to the mini or small restaurant owners being the least qualified. Among the priests, 39 per cent have undergraduate qualification whereas 13 per cent belong to under-matric category. As high as 70 per cent among Pooja Samagri vendors are qualified from undergraduate level to graduate and above while 30 per cent are under matriculates. While a fifth of the shoe stand owners are found to be graduates and above, interestingly, number of shoe-stand owners are found to be graduates and above. Interestingly, equal number of shoe-stand owners are found to be under matriculates and undergraduates. Though a higher percentage of 56 among the photographers do have a graduate qualification and above the same for undergraduates and under matriculates stand at 28 and 6 per cent respectively. Nearly 27 and 18 per cent among the cold-drink vendors are under graduates and above whereas a high percentage of 56 happens to be under matriculates. Similarly a third among the Nolias are found to be under matriculates. Whereas , 47 and 20 per cent among them are undergraduates and graduates and above respectively. Equal number of boatmen seems to be under matriculates and undergraduates while 23 per cent among them are graduates and above. Furthermore, stationery shop owners are mostly (56%) with graduate qualification and above while 21 and 23 per cent of them are under-matriculates and under graduates respectively. Almost a fifth among the peddlers are found to he under and above matriculation while 29 and 52 per cent among them are seen to be under matriculates and under graduates respectively.

Hardly a fifth among the beetle shop owners are found to have graduation or higher qualification while a fifth and significantly 59 per cent of them are seem to be under matriculates and under graduates respectively. Whereas 60 per cent among the handicraft stall owners seem to be undergraduates. Only 15 per cent prove to be under matriculates. Noticeably 42 per cent of the entertainers are under matriculates while a fourth and a third seem to be under graduates and above.

Table 2.4: Respondent Qualifications

Sl. No.	Vocation	Under matric		Under Graduates		Graduates above		Total	
		No	%	No	%	No	%	No	%
1.	Priest	21	13.46	61	39.10	74	47.44	156	100
2.	Pooja material	16	29.4	25	45.45	14	25.46	55	100
3.	Shoe stand	06	40.0	06	40.0	03	20.0	15	100
4.	Photography	04	16.0	07	28.0	14	56	25	100
5.	Guide	02	10.0	06	30	12	60	20	100
6.	Drinks	25	55.55	12	26.67	08	17.78	45	100
7.	Nolia	05	33.33	07	46.67	03	20	15	100
8.	Boating	08	38.09	08	38.09	05	23.82	21	100
9.	Restaurant	06	13.63	10	23.07	28	63.67	44	100
10.	Stationaryshop	11	21.15	12	52.38	29	55.78	52	100
11.	Peddlers	12	28.57	22	20.45	08	19.05	42	100
12.	Bettle shop	26	59.09	09	59.68	09	20.43	44	100
13.	Handicraft	09	14.51	37	36.36	16	25.81	62	100
14.	PCOs	02	09.09	08	36.4	12	54.55	22	100
15.	Entertainment	05	41.66	03	25.0	04	33.34	12	100
16.	**Total**	**141**	**22.38**	**250**	**39.68**	**239**	**37.94**	**630**	**100**

Source: Primary Data Collected.

Turnover

Monthly turnover in case of nearly 40 per cent among the priests ranges between Rs. 5000 to Rs. 10,000 whereas little over a fourth among them stand to earn more than Rs. 10,000. More than one third of the priests' income comes within Rs. 5000 bracket. The same one-third among boat men and entertainers also find their turnover in this bracket. Whereas, more than a Half of the boatmen fetch a turnover between Rs. 5,000 to Rs. 10,000 and a minority of 14 per cent receive a turnover above of Rs. 10,000. In contrast, no entertainer is found to register a turnover above Rs. 10,000 while that of little over 66 per cent of them falls between Rs. 5,000 to Rs. 10,000.

Above 40 per cent of the restaurant proprietors register a turnover between Rs. 5,000 to Rs. 10.000, whereas, almost 32 per cent and about 27 per cent among them fetch a turnover of Rs. 5,000 to Rs.10,000 and above Rs. 10,000 respectively. Half of the stationary shop owners, those who invest at par with the restaurant owners are found to bag a turnover between Rs. 5000 to Rs. 10,000 while little more than 21 per cent and nearly 29 per cent among them earn upto Rs. 5000 and above Rs. 10.000 respectively. However in case of the PCO's turnover stand differently. Nearly 46 per cent fall in the category of up to Rs. 5000. Almost 41 per cent earning between Rs.5, 000 to Rs. 10,000 while more than 13 per cent earn beyond Rs.10,000. The handicraft stall owners sometimes with big investments in the business indicate a turnover pattern promoting the artists' effort. As a result, 48 per cent among them secure a turnover of Rs. 10,000 and above.

Noticeably, as high as 60 per cent among the Guides, Nólias and puja material vendors earth a monthly turnover up to Rs. 5,000.

None of the Nolias is able to make a turnover beyond Rs. 10,000 which is only 10 and 11 per cent among the guides and Pooja Samagri vendors respectively whose turnover reaches above Rs. 10,000. The rest among both the occupants are found to fetch between Rs. 5,000 to 10,000. It is also observed that not less than 40 per cent among the photographers make up to Rs. 5,000 turn over. Across all the occupants, both peddlers and battle shop owners stand at a majority in the turnover bracket Rs.5,000 to Rs. 10,000. But none of the peddler is found in the last category, *i.e.*, beyond Rs. 10,000. A very negligible, *i.e.*, 45 per cent of Bettle shop owners cross the turnover of Rs. 10,000 mark. However, similar trend is observed among the drink vendors.

Monthly Income

Monthly income, an important measure of the occupants economic health consists of three groups. Which are reflected in Table 2.5 . It is noteworthy to record that 76 per cent among the peddlers earn between Rs. 4,000 to Rs.6,000 per month.

Table 2.5: Monthly Income

Sl. No.	Vocational Occupant	2000-4000 %		4000-6000 %		6000 and above%		Total No %	
1.	Priest	35	22.4	60	38.5	61	39.1	156	100
2.	Pooja material	10	29.4	11	32.4	34	38.2	55	100
3.	Shoe stand	05	33.3	06	40	04	26.7	15	100
4.	Photography	06	24	13	50	07	25	26	100
5.	Guide	04	20	06	30	10	50	20	100
6.	Drinks	09	20	24	53.3	12	26.7	45	100
7.	Nolia	06	40	07	46.7	02	13.3	15	100
8.	Boatman	02	9.5	04	19	15	71.5	21	100
9.	Restaurant	12	27.3	09	20.5	23	52.2	44	100
10.	Stationaryshop	09	17.3	24	46.2	19	36.5	52	100
11.	peddlers	06	14.3	32	76.2	04	9.5	42	100
12.	Bettle shop	12	27.3	20	45.5	12	27.2	44	100
13.	Handicraft	07	11.3	25	40.3	30	48.4	62	100
14.	PCOs	07	31.8	08	36.4	07	31.8	22	100
15.	Entertainment	02	16.7	06	50	04	33.3	12	100
16.	**Total**	**132**	**40.3**	**254**	**38.7**	**249**	**38.7**	**630**	**100**

Source: Primary Data Collected

While only a tenth among them and the boatmen earn above Rs. 6,000 and between two to four thousand respectively. However as high as 72 per cent of the boatmen earn above Rs.6,000. The monthly income of half of the guides goes beyond Rs. 6,000, whereas a fifth among the guides and drink-venders earn between Rs, 2 to 4 thousands per month. An encouraging figure of about 40 per cent among the priests and Puja material vendors earn beyond Rs. 6,000 due to a favourable and tourist attractive place of their vocation. However, 40 and 27 per cent among the shoe- stand owners earn between 4 to 6 thousand and above 6 thousands respectively. The income of half of the photographers is between Rs 4,000 to Rs.6,000 while almost a fourth each earn between Rs 2 to 4 thousand and Rs. 6 thousand. 40 per cent of Nolias, the most poverty- striken among the 15 groups of vocational occupants , earn between Rs 2 to 4 thousand about 27 per cent among the restaurant owners earn between Rs. 2-4 thousand and a majority of them receive beyond Rs. 6 thousand. Both handicraft and stationary vendors nearly half of them earn an income of about Rs 6 thousand.

Encouragement to Children to Adopt the Vocation

Table 2.6 shows the number and percentage of vocational occupants interested for their own children to continue their vocation. Most significant among them, *i e.*, three-fourth of the entertainers reject the vocation to be occupied by their own children. However, 52 per cent among handicraft stall owners refuse their children to adopt the vocation. Nearly 28 per cent among the priest interest to accept of the occupation by their children while about 73 per cent refuse. Among the puja material vendors little more than a third reply in affirmative whereas twice of that reply negatively. Similarly, as high as 73 per cent say no for inheriting the vocation by their children while the remaining show their preference for the same. Further, 40 per cent each among the guides, drink vendors and Nolias give a positive reply and the rest say no. Photographers (44%) answer affirmatively while 56 per cent say no to it. Even 57 per cent among the boat men and 68 per cent restaurant owners with comparatively higher investment in their vocation answer negatively. Likewise, both stationery shop and handicraft stall owners making a sizable investment opening positive stand at 27 per cent and 48 per cent respectively.

In case of the peddlers and beetle shop owners, 71 to 73 per cent give a negative reply for inheritance by their children while 68 per cent among the PCO proprietors also disapprove and reject such inheritance. Mostly, it is found that one third across all the occupants give their assent for their children to accept the vocation and two third reject the same.

Table 2.6: Encouragement to Children to Adopt the Vocation

Sl. No	Vocational occupants	Yes		No		Total	
		No	%	No	%	No	%
1.	Priest	43	27.56	113	72.54	156	100
2.	Pooja materials	19	34.54	36	65.46	55	100
3.	Shoe stand	4	26.67	11	73.34	25	100
4.	Photography	11	44	14	56	15	100
5.	Guide	8	40	12	60	20	100
6.	Drinks	18	40	27	60	45	100
7.	Nolia	6	40	09	60	15	100
8.	Boatman	9	42.9	12	57.1	21	100
9.	Restaurant	14	31.8	30	68.2	44	100
10.	Stationaryshop	14	26.9	38	73.1	52	100
11.	Peddlers	12	28.6	30	71.4	42	100
12.	Bettle shop	12	27.27	32	72.73	44	100
13.	Handicraft	30	48.4	32	51.6	62	100
14.	PCOs	07	31.8	15	68.2	22	100
15.	Entertainment	03	25.0	09	75.0	12	100
16.	**Total**	**210**	**33.33**	**420**	**66.67**	**630**	**100**

Source: Primary Data Collected.

Level of Satisfaction

The respondents were asked to rate their level of satisfaction from their respective vocations. The summery of their opinions as presented in Table 2.7. Reveals that none of the respondents are highly satisfied in their vocations. It is also significant to note that none of the respondents expressed moderate satisfaction from their vocations. The mean score is below 3.0 for all vocations excepting two vocations that is photography and restaurants. The average score is just above 3 *i.e.* 3.1 in both the cases. Some vocations, i.e., shoe stand, guides, Nolia and boatmen, express almost dissatisfaction from their jobs as the mean score for these vocations is less than 2.0.

Table 2.7: Level of Satisfaction

Sl. No.	Vocational occupants	Mean	Standard deviation
1.	Priest	2.5	.014
2.	Pooja materials	2.6	.021
3.	Shoe stand	1.8	.013
4.	Photography	3.1	.012
5.	Guide	1.8	.013
6.	Drinks	2.4	.012
7.	Nolia	1.9	.014
8.	Boatmen	1.8	.013
9.	Restaurant	3.1	0.14
10.	Stationary shop	2.9	.020
11.	Peddlers	2.2	.011
12.	Bettle shop	2.6	.014
13.	Handicraft	2.8	.015
14.	PCOs	1.8	.015
15.	Entertainment	1.2	.020
16.	**Total**	**2.35**	**22.38**

At the lower end of the satisfaction, we also find the vocation like, priests, Puja Material vendors, Drinks, Handicrafts, stationary shops etc.

Further, we observe that the respondent's opinions are not totally unbiased. They present varying opinion, often contradictory in nature. However, the trend of the level of satisfaction is clear and creates a scope for devising means of strengthening their vocations with a view to raise their level of satisfaction. The overall average score of satisfaction level is 2.35 which signifies less than moderate satisfaction and higher than level of dissatisfaction. This kind of opinion was also expected from them as many expressed pessimism over continuing or improving the vocation.

Factors Responsible for Decline of the Vocation

Finally, the views of various respondents in tourism vocations were sought regarding the factors chiefly responsible for the decline of the vocation. Interestingly it was observed that majority of the respondents attributed insufficient earning as the most significant factor. While they attributed their dissatisfaction to the lack of communication and amenities available at the tourist centres. The next important factor was highlighted as to the polluted environment. Absence of proper sanitation and security were considered detrimental to the tourism vocations at various tourist places. The next significant factor in order of the weightage happened to be non- cooperation of the Government agencies for the development of tourism and related vocations.

The above responses of the tourism entrepreneurs are corroborated by the degree of level of satisfaction in their respective vocations as presented in Table 2.7 of the study. However, the respondents were not prepared to accept some of the other factors such as high cost of vocation, fall in tourist inflows and disinterest of the tourists which may be responsible for the decline of the vocation.

Conclusion

Undoubtedly, tourism in coastal Odisha has emerged as an activity leading to the number of socio-economic benefits. The expenditure made by the tourists at various tourist places leaves a multiplier effect on the overall economy of the region. At the same time, large scale unemployment and ever increasing poverty in the State of Odisha underscore the need for tapping tourism resource and exploring new avenues of tourist interests. Besides, infrastructural development in the region, it also creates employment opportunities for the prospective tourism entrepreneurs. Being a service sector, tourism vocation offers employment to both the semi-skilled as well as unskilled local unemployed population.

Population of Odisha constitutes 3.57 per cent of Indian population. Out of them, 85 per cent live in rural areas mostly depending an agriculture. But the annual expenditure of the State have always been out stripping its annual income over the years. Growing unemployment, particularly the educated unemployed youth, is one of the baffling problems faced by the state. The rich natural and human resources in odisha offer a huge potential for development of tourism industry and its related vocations. In fact, tourism is looked upon to provide a vast innovative scope for development of several vocations. Besides, nature of employment skilled and unskilled, seasonal and perennial provided by tourism is found to be significant. Majority among vocational occupiers in coastal Odisha tourist places are either unskilled or semi-skilled. Moreover, tourism provides indirect employment to many rural people outside the industry, *i.e.*, those who provide goods and services to those directly engaged in the industry.

The holy state of Odisha occupies a prominent position in the tourist map of India. Endowed with some of India's best kept culture secrets from the outside world, Odisha offers a multidimensional experience spanning rich architectural monuments, a golden coast line, wild life, art and craft. As a result, Odisha tourism not only attracts domestic tourists but also international tourists. The State having all the favourable potentialities, due attention should be given by the planners, policy makers as well as by the Governments of State as well as Centre for the development of tourism sector in order to achieve the State's economic growth by reducing the BPL population and empowering rural Odisha.

References

1. Aghion, P.N. Bloom, R. Blundell, R. Griffith and P. Howitt (2005) "Competition and Innovation an Inverted U-relationship *Quarterly Journal of Economics* 120 (2).
2. Alesina A. and D. Rodrik (1994) "Distributive Policies and Economic Growth" *Quarterly Journal of Economic* 109.
3. Barro, R. 2000 "Inequality and Growth in a Panel of Countries" *Journal of Economic Growth* 5.

4. Commission on Growth and Development (2008), Growth Report: Strategies for Sustained Growth and Inclusive Development, the World Bank.

5. *World Bank Economic Review* 10, pp. 565-91.

6. *The Economic Survey,* 2009-10.

7. Sussex : Institute of Development Studies OECD (2008) Growing Unequal? Income Distribution and Poverty in OECD Countries.

8. Sida (2006), Integrated Economic Analysis for Pro-poor Growth: A Methodological Approach Method Document, Stockholm: Sida.

Women Entrepreneurship *Problems and Perspectives*

Dr. Veerashetty G, Rathod
Dr. Vithob B, Dr. Srikant

Introduction

India has secured the second place in the world having highest population, out of the total population, half of the population covered by women, constitute the largest group which is excluded from the benefits of development. In India, the work participation rate of women is less compared to men. The multiple roles of women and the meager ability to access resources and available assets are areas of concern. It is important to emphasize that women require adequate security and protection to be self-reliant. Among women, widows are the most vulnerable sections of the society. Several studies have pointed out that female widowhood in India tends to be associated with economic deprivation. Yet the amelioration of the socio-economic condition widows in India has not been given due consideration at the level of the Central Government. Some state governments have introduced special pension schemes fort widows, but the rates of pension schemes, as they exist today, can be said to be effective instrument of social security to women. The Ninth Five-year plan adopted the strategy of women's component plan under which not less than 30 per cent of funds or benefits are earmarked in all the women related sectors for women specific programmes. The Tenth Five-year plan has undertaken to further strengthen the process of women's component plan.

The role of women in Indian society is vital. Apart from the matriarchal society, women play a decisive role in most of the patriarchal societies also. The future of children depends, by and large, upon the mothers who generally stays at home and take care of children's health and education. This is particularly so in countries like India where society and life of people are molded by traditional and spiritual foundations. The status of women in Indian economy is either unorganized or at least undervalued. The economic status of the women is generally weak, which is a matter of great concern. Though, the Constitution of India guarantees various types of equalities to women. Even though, Government of India has not concern fully for their socio-economic development. Government is making some of the policies for the development of women but it does not reach the poor generally and particularly women belong to weaker section. India has made considerable progress in socio-economic development in recent decades, as improvement in indicators such as life expectancy, infant mortality, maternal mortality, literacy and employment etc. However, India has lagging behind in improving the status of women. The present chapter is highlighted the women empowerment through the entrepreneurship in India.

Objectives

The study has many objectives as follows:

1. To study the concept and role of entrepreneurship in the enlistment of women status;
2. To examine the work participation rate in India;
3. To study the growth women entrepreneurship in India;
4. To analyse the problems and prospects of women entrepreneurship.

Methodology

The present study is based on secondary data only; this data's collected from various books, journals, government reports, published and unpublished research thesis and various webs. After collected of the secondary data were tabulated in the form of simple percentage.

Concept of Entrepreneurship

Entrepreneurship means, different things to different people. However in spite of differences there are some common aspects. In 1961 Schumpeter defined entrepreneur as "a dynamic agent of change, or the catalyst who transforms increasingly natural and human resources into correspondingly production possibilities." They are effective leaders calculated risk takers, creative perceiver of new marketing opportunity and can manage their financial affairs.

Women in Un-organized Sector

The presence of vast multitudes of women as workers and producers in the unorganized sector, where earnings are low, employment seasonal and insecure, supportive services woefully inadequate or even non-existent, growth opportunities few and collective organization weak, has brought into sharp focus the failure of the mainstream alleviate their predicament. What is true that workers, irrespective of sex, are exploited in the unorganized sector, women suffer more by the fact of their gender. There is enough evidence substantiate that developmental processes have only pushed women to states of survival. Until recently, their contribution to the economy through self employed and home based has gone unnoticed. The national database pays little attention to their presence or contribution. It is only in the past decade and a half that there has been some recognition of the fact that self-employed and home-based workers are part of the labour force. According to National Commission on Self Employed Women estimates that 94 per cent of the total female work force is to be found in unorganized sector understood by the following table.

Table 3.1: Distribution of Female Workers in India 1961 to 2001

Census year	Cultivators	Agriculture labours	House-hold	Industry & Other service	% of female workers to total female population
1961	15.47	6.83	2.13	3.47	27.9
1971	3.06	6.13	0.51	1.82	12.06
1981	4.65	6.46	0.64	2.24	13.99
1991	5.49	7.20	0.57	2.77	16.30
2001	8.35	10.12	1.63	5.57	25.67

Source: Statistical Profile on Women Labour, p. 4.

The above table reveals that, the unorganized labours are increasing by census to census and in 2001 census all categories have increased when compared to 1991 census. The percentage of female workers to total female population is 25.67 in 2001 census. It is increased by 16.30 per cent in 1991 census.

In the organized and unorganized sector works were based on females, and most of the jobs are reserved for female laborers in both sector, though work participation by sex is very low than male may be understood by the below table.

Table 3.2: Work Participation Rate by Sex in India

Census Year	Persons	Male	Female
1971	33.06	52.61	12.06
1981	36.70	52.62	19.67
1991	37.50	51.61	22.27
2001	39.26	51.93	25.68

Source:
1. Census of India. 1971 part II B (I), statement 8.
2. Census of India. 1981 & 1991 part II B (I) Vol. II, Statement-9.
3. Census of India 2001, Haryana provisional population totals paper 3.

Note:
1. Excludes Assam where the 1981 census could not be held and Jammu & Kashmir where the 1991 census could not be held.
2. The 1971 census figures include workers and non-workers with secondary work. The 1981 and 1991 census figure includes main workers and marginal workers.

The above table shows that, the work participation rate is worst of female from 1971 to 2001 in India, from these four decades the female work participation rate less than male labourers. In 1971 the female rate is 12.06 and male rate is 52.16. But it is slightly improved in 2001 census *i.e.*, 25.68 of female and 51.93 is male labourers, because globalization has supported to female population for improved their economic conditions in the society and also they have sustained by them self in participating the various economic activities such as self employment through SHGs and Stree Shakti Programmes in India.

Growth of Women Entrepreneurs

In present scenario regarding women entrepreneurship in India, we do not have the figures to show how many women's are working as a entrepreneurs and how many women enterprises are in operation either in country or in any of the states. So it is very difficult to assess the development women entrepreneurship in India. Some rough data for three states indicates that there are about 1000 women enterprises in Karnataka, 700 in Gujarat and 500 in Tamil Nadu. It will be affair generation that while women constitute about 50 per cent of our population, the proportion of enterprises set up and run by women is a fraction of one per cent.

Constraints Which Prevent Women to Becoming Entrepreneurs

There are five critical constraints which prevent potential entrepreneurs whether men or women from becoming actual entrepreneurs.

1. Lack of confidence and motivation;
2. Lack of knowledge about business opportunities;
3. Lack of information regarding how to go about formulating a business plan including market survey;
4. Lack of information about procedures and sources of assistance including finance;
5. Lack of knowledge about how to manage ones own enterprise.

Three Distinct Situations Emerge Which are Specially Supports to Women to Become Entrepreneurs

(i) *Chance Entrepreneurs:* Where they went into business without any preparation, clear goals or plans.

(ii) *Forced Entrepreneurs:* Compelled by circumstances such as death of husband or father with responsibilities falling on them to take over the existing business.

(iii) *Created Entrepreneurs:* Located, motivated, encouraged and developed through Entrepreneurs Development Programmes, as a part of strategy to develop women as a competent entrepreneurs.

Problems Faced by Women Entrepreneurs

The problems faced by women entrepreneurs in India can be classified in different categories, which are:

A. General/Personal Problems

1. Absence of sense of need for achievement
2. Excessive burden of work and responsibility of family affairs, child and husband care
3. Lack of leisure time and other activity
4. Tendency to avoid economic risk, social risk, technical and environmental risk
5. Lack of emotional maturity in dealing with business situation
6. Lack of entrepreneurial initiative due to lack of confidence
7. Lack self-image and self-esteem

B. Educational Problems

1. Lack of education particularly technical education
2. Lack of knowledge of agencies and institutions assisting entrepreneurs
3. Lack of knowledge of various schemes run by government

4. Lack of knowledge of different law/legal aspects, and
5. Lack of knowledge of loan schemes procedures of financial institutions.

C. Social Problems

1. Lack of motivation
2. Lack of motivation from family and society
3. Conflict due to dual responsibilities
4. Non co-operative attitude of husband and family members
5. No appreciation for independent decisions
6. Lack of recognition and appreciation in the family
7. Male dominance
8. Lack of social contacts
9. Lack of confidence in women's ability

D. Economic/Financial Problems

1. Lack of availability of loan facilities
2. Lack of own funds and financial resources
3. Limited working capital
4. Constant need of finances
5. Ignorance of banking procedures and formalities due to illiteracy
6. Delay in payment of bills
7. Economic incredibility of women
8. Lack of collateral security
9. Non-availability of agency to guide and advice, on identification of investment opportunities
10. Lack of knowledge of accounting

E. Technological Problems

1. Lack of technical know how about running the unit
2. Lack of specialized skill to work on specific projects due to in competency

3. Unable to work in project round the year
4. Lack of facilities for communicating with women entrepreneurs about the development and availability of modern technologies
5. Difficulty in maintenance and repair of machinery

F. **Raw Material Problems**

1. Non-availability of required inputs
2. Lack of supply of raw material for uninterrupted production
3. Time consuming procedures of procurement of raw material
4. Variations in raw material prices at different places
5. Lack of sufficient stock of raw material in period of short supply and price change due to poor inventory management

G. **Marketing Problems**

1. Lack of marketing experience and poor knowledge of market
2. Competition from established and larger units
3. Delayed disposal of products due to in adequate sales promotional avenues and lack of contract with middleman
4. Difficulty in getting money from buyer after sale
5. Lack of sufficient finished goods for smooth sales operation and efficient customer service

H. **Managerial Problems**

1. Lack of clear-cut objectives
2. Lack of planning
3. Poor management
4. Poor project implementation
5. Lack of decision-making

6. Incompetent in handling technical, financial, sale and manufacturing activities
7. Lack of adequate research facilities
8. Lack of managerial kill

I. Infrastructural Problems

1. In adequate power supply
2. In adequate water supply
3. Lack of communication facilities
4. Delays in provision of infrastructural facilities, like land, Shedds, Plots, premises etc.
5. Lack of adequate and proper information system

J. Support System Problems

1. In adequate incentives
2. Complicated procedures and formalities result in delays sanction of assistance
3. Non co-operative attitude of the employees
4. Political influences need to avail timely institutional help
5. Bribery in the agencies providing subsidies/incentives/ loans
6. Lack of effective communication between field functionaries and women entrepreneurs
7. Lack of communication and co-ordination between different agencies
8. Arrestment in completion of document and other formalities

K. Manpower Support Problems

1. Insufficient staff to carry out project successfully
2. Non-availability of skilled workers
3. Experienced workers leave the unit after sufficient exposure

Government and NGOs for the Development of Women Entrepreneurs

A number of organizations and institutions of central and state governments and non government organizations have been offering a variety of programmes, incentives, facilities for the promotion and development entrepreneurship among women in India, which have been discussed in following.

Small Industries Development Bank of India (SIDBI), besides providing finance to small enterprises also undertakes following development activities:

1. Technology upgrade and management development;
2. Creativity promotion;
3. Government management;
4. Staff up gradation and management development;
5. Entrepreneurial development;
6. Marketing and export promotion;
7. Rural industries;
8. Economic improvement of women;
9. Information dissemination.

National Small Industries Corporation (NSIC), Small Industries Development Organization (SIDC) and National Research Development Corporation of India (NRDC) help women by providing:

1. Assistance to small scale industries with some special programmes and schemes for the promotion and development of women entrepreneurship in the country;
2. Organizing of training programmes for the development of women entrepreneurs in India.

Khadi and Village Industries Commission (KVIC), Central Social Welfare Board (CSWB), National Institute of Entrepreneurship and Small Business Development (NIESBUD), National Alliance of Young Entrepreneurs

(NAYE), District Industry Center (DIC), National Institute for Small Industry Extension and Training (NISIET) were established with one of their objectives as conducting conferences, symposia, and workshops to discuss problems of women entrepreneur in India.

State Financial Corporation (SFC), Women Co-operative Finance Corporation (WCFC) and other nationalized banks are playing important role in promoting self-employment among women by making available credit facilities with number of concessions and 20 per cent subsidy. Beside, under Nehru Rozgar Yojana Sch, banks are provide 75 per cent of the funds and 25 per cent of the funds are provided by WCFC.

State-wise Organizations

In Assam the organizations, *viz.*, SISI, NISIET, NETTCO, ASIDC, AIDC, AHSIDC, AFC, DHC, etc., organize entrepreneurship development programmes for the development of women entrepreneurship. CEDMAP in Madya Pradesh organize training programmes in various parts of the state for all sections of society, designed to suit the local people for identifying local resources products and technology. In Andra Pradesh, NIRD, NISIFT, SISI, SIDBI, have come forward to guide, help and stimulate the movement of women entrepreneurs. The institutions, *viz.* SBI, IDBI and APSFC are coming forward to provide assistance to women entrepreneurs in the state of Andra Pradesh.

In Kerala according to a study, the number of women's industrial units was 358 in 1981, which rose to 782 in 1984. These 782 units included 592 proprietary firms, 43 partnerships firms, 42 charitable institutions, joint stock companies and 102 co-operative societies. Proper education of women in Kerala resulted in high motivation. The success of women entrepreneurs in Kerala, who returning their own entrepreneurship among the Muslim women entrepreneurs in utterly lacking due religious and cultural constraints.

Apart from the above a number of institutes and organizations *viz.*, the Institute of Management Development and Research in Pune, Centre for Management Development in Kerala, New Delhi Polytechnic for Women, Bihar Electronic Development Corporation, Science and Technology of Development of Union Government, Entrepreneurship Dev. Institutions of India (EDII), Allahabad, Technical Teacher Training Institute Chandigarh, Institute for Entrepreneurship Development in Uttar Pradesh, MP, Rajastan, Haryana, Punjab, Himachal Pradesh and Jammu and Kashmir are actively involved in the promotion and development of women entrepreneurship all over the country.

Suggestions

1. To organize a number of training programmes especially for women in grassroot level, it helps women to gain more knowledge about how to develop entrepreneurship;
2. To make advertisement through media in such way that information about programmese and schemes sponsored by the government for the development of entrepreneurship is to reach the rural poor generally, particularly to women;
3. To prevent corruption at the time of providing benefits to beneficiaries through programmes and schemes for the development of women entrepreneurship;
4. To change implementing mechanism of policies and programmes.

Conclusion

Women occupied large part of the total population in India. Although women logging behind in many aspects *viz.*, educational, economical, social cultural etc. When we talk about women entrepreneurship, women are facing number of problems, *viz.*, general/personal problems, educational problems, financial problems, managerial problems, support system problems, infrastructural problems, etc. For improving existing performance of women entrepreneurs central and state governments implemented large number of programmes and schemes but not succeed up to the mark.

References

1. Ramaswamy Uma, (1991), "Women and Development," *The Indian Journal of Labour Economics*, Vol. 34, No. 3, pp. 211-220.
2. Raman, N.C. (1999), "Indian Women Entrepreneurial Potential," Raju.V.B. Girija. (Eds) (1999), " Small Enterprise Views and Vistas," Silver Jubilee Commemorative Special, Tata McGraw, Hill Publications Company limited, New Delhi.
3. Sumi Guha—Entrepreneurship and Empowerment of Women.
4. Mehfooz Ur Rahmam, Yasser Mehfooz and Ziauddin Khairoowala, — Women Entrepreneurs in India: Problems and Prospects.
5. S.K. Dhameja, R.S. Bhatia and J.S. Sinai,— Women Entrepreneurs: Perceptions, Attitudes and Opinion.
6. Dr. Poonam Singh, — Status and Role of Rural Women in India.
7. Dr. Meenu Agarwal, — Empowerment of women in India.
8. Dr. Ramesh Madan, — Empowerment of Rural Women and New Millennium.
9. Dr. Upasna Sharma, — Rural Women's Work Participation in India.
10. Dr. V.G. Patel, — Women Entrepreneurship Development.
11. N.C. Raman, — Indian Women and Entrepreneurial Potential.

Sustainopreneurship—Business with a Cause
An Overview

Dr. Sushil K. Pattanaik,
Dr. S.K. Das

ABSTRACT

The tentative definition of the concept of sustainopreneurship — in the most simplified form described as entrepreneurship and innovation for sustainability — "Business with a Cause". The concept takes its departure from generic entrepreneurship theory development, its extensions and further contextualization into the domains of sustainability, primarily through recent research. A literature review provides core references related to the conceptualization of sustainability entrepreneurship. A claim is made that there is a need for further conceptual development, especially viewed in contrast to the empirical material and experience, when digesting the literature that deals with concepts preceding sustainopreneurship. These concepts are eco-preneurship and social entrepreneurship, as well as current descriptions of sustainability entrepreneurship, including some sources where the word sustainopreneurship in itself is introduced for the first time. The methodological approach used when conducting the literature review is an analytical stance. Additional analysis, integrating and extending the reviewed sources, leads us to a performative definition of sustainopreneurship. This tentative definition is presented as an imagined prospective wordbook entry in a "future history" format. One of the key distinctions in between entre-preneurship in general and sustainopreneurship, is that sustainopreneurship is mission—and cause oriented-business activity is used as a means to solve sustainability-related problems. In short, to turn business activity from being a part of the problem to be a part of the solution.

Entrepreneurship—The Common Theory

Entrepreneurship is popular in the society, claim to give success in the process, aiming to a positive societal development. The overall wonder in this case, to *e.g.* eradicate poverty or create the sustainable world by contributing towards a positive process of prosperity creation and empowerment on individual, family and (local) community level and an efficient means to solve sustainability related problems. In this context, it can be a strong potential contributor in this process, as an enabler. With this approach, we make this conceptual review, which also moves to the point where the aspect of positive social change gets strengthened when taken to the sustainability context, in line with the purposes and the background motives. These are:

- Sustainability stability
- Innovation creativity
- Entrepreneurship power to act
- Endurance patience humility joy
- Inspiration credibility transparency
- Enabler norm creator awareness
- Change dialogue respect
- Agility integrity
- Realization results

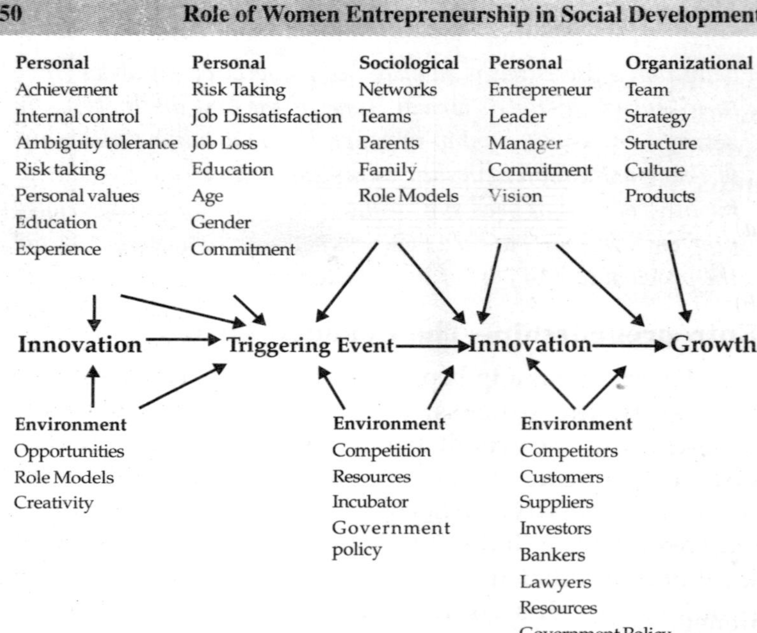

Fig. 4.1: **Moving Dimensions along with risk and Uncertainty in Entrepreneurships**

Source: The Entrepreneurial Events Formation Process. Source: Bygrave, 1989, p. 9.

Extending the Concept

There is an increasing number of voices to view the entrepreneurship phenomenon as something more than just having entrepreneurship and entrepreneurs associated with the economical context, to rather see it as a social phenomenon. The community entrepreneur is begin with the entrepreneur-in-economics as land—an entrepreneur who creates entrepreneurial possibilities, opportunities and environments for others, contributing to entrepreneurial spirit, and transforming local communities ... Related to the concept of community is also the 'civic entrepreneur', moving in the boundary of the own firm and its own economic activities, in the firm clusters of the economy sphere. An entrepreneur in collective attempt to build up new collective identities and regaining leadership at grassroots levels to revamp the whole community with mobilising its competencies. A systematic overview of all the new openings and widening of the entrepreneurship concept collects all new facets of an entrepreneurship discourse by widening the three dimensions:

(a) *Societal*—reclaiming entrepreneurship as a societal phenomenon, not primarily economic;

(b) *Place/space*—to research entrepreneurship in 'odd' contexts not represented before;

(c) *Discursive spaces*—bringing in social sciences and humanities more systematic.

One of the suggested consequences is e.g. liberating it from 'entrepreneur-as-hero' stories and bringing in everydayness entrepreneurship, *e.g.* the homeless selling umbrellas in the case of rain. To give a contemporary view of the entrepreneur-as-societal phenomenon. From entrepreneurship, a number of combinations from sources have been classified as:

- Public entrepreneurship
- Therapists entrepreneurship
- Ethnic entrepreneurship
- Artisan entrepreneurship
- Health sector entrepreneurship
- Informal third world entrepreneurship
- Ecological entrepreneurship
- NGO entrepreneurship
- Civic entrepreneurship
- Education/university entrepreneurship
- City entrepreneurship
- Social entrepreneurship

Entrepreneurship Towards the Context of Sustainability

The business community has the contributions towards a sustainable world. In addition to integrating across fields, sustainability must also be integrated across sectors or interests. It is clear that governments alone have neither the will nor the capability to accomplish sustainability on their own. The private sector, as the engine of economic activity on the planet, and a major source for creativity, innovation and entrepreneurship, Further, entrepreneurship towards the sustainability context, the role of social entrepreneurship for the preservation and positive development of the basic infrastructure is most vital.

Sustainability Entrepreneurship

All the aspects have been created and added to the multi-faceted concept of entrepreneurship with these extensions and new connections with ecological and social as new tags, still leaves us unsatisfied when brought to the sustainability context. There is a risk of treating these kinds of specific categories of entrepreneurial behaviours to miss the holistic, integrated approach implied by the sustainability paradigm. Taking together sustainability with entrepreneurship invites us to a new strand of conversation. In this dialogue we try to grasp the phenomenon where we use business organizing as a means to create solutions and opportunities of the agenda imposed by the movements created by the sustainable development discourse. The keyword to guide us further is *integration* — to integrate social, ecological and economical aspects with entrepreneurial behaviour.

Sustainability Imperatives

To build a context for these trajectories further on and to move them ahead in order to integrate all dimensions of sustainability. These has been suggested a three-dimensional 'imperative' of sustainability, *i.e.* what sustainability requires that in a sense could be a verbal translation of the 'target board model':

- The ecological imperative is to stay within the biophysical carrying capacity of the planet;
- The economic imperative is to provide an adequate material standard of living of all;
- The social imperative is to provide systems of governance that propagate the values that people want to live by.

Sustainability Innovation

It is any process of social change which increases the proceeds derived from current natural, social, and economic capital, while at the same time protecting and enhancing the underlying capital stock.

In a nut shell, Sustainability Entrepreneurship consists of the identification of a sustainability innovation and its implementation either through the foundation of a start-up or the radical reorientation of an existing organization's business model so as to achieve the underlying ecological or social objectives.

Sustainable *vs.* Sustainability Entrepreneurship

Sustainable entrepreneurship attaching an attribute to the 'generic' entrepreneurial process. Sustainability requires 'and', as in *'ecological and social objectives'*—the integrated meaning that follows from and is implied by the sustainability approach. If only one of the two optional dimensions besides the economical 'entrepreneurships—usual' is present, then it would reflect the case more clear to stick to either eco-preneurship or social entrepreneurship, respectively. Sustainability entrepreneurship—by forming the concept *sustainopreneurship;* the use of entrepreneurial activity in a *determined action orientation towards solving a sustainability-related problem* with business organising as a means to solve the problem(s) — *'business with a cause':* To turn business activity from a part of the problem to a part of the solution.

Sustainopreneurship—A Tentative Definition

It can be defined as:

1. Deployment of sustainability innovations: *Entrepreneurship and innovation for sustainability.*
2. Short for sustainability intra-/entrepreneurship.
3. To focus on one or more (world/social/sustainability related) problem(s), find/identify and/or invent a solution to the problem(s) and bring the innovation to the market by creating an efficient organisation. With the (deep transformation of an old) mission/cause oriented sustainability business created, adding ecological/economical/social values and gains, with a bias towards the intangible— through dematerialization/resocialisation. The value added at the same time preserving, restoring and/or ultimately enhancing the underlying utilized capital stock, in order to maintain the capacity to fulfil the needs of present and coming generations of stakeholders.

Core Dimensions of Sustainopreneurship

To summarize: Sustainopreneurship, with this definition, highlights three distinguishing dimensions, all three are present simultaneously in the interaction it reflects.

1. Seeking, finding and/or creating innovations to solve sustainability-related problems and innovative solutions to the problems related to the sustainability agenda.
2. Getting solutions to the market through creative organizing.

In this dimension, sustainopreneurship is a conceptual extension and development from the social phenomenon named entrepreneurship, and thus inherits one of its perceived key dimensions, 'entrepreneurship as creative organizing'. Market is used, as well, not society primarily, since it implies business establishment — a sustainability business that still knows its place and role in the holarchy. Bringing something to the market, at the same time brings it to society and the environment.

3. Adding sustainability value with respect for life support systems.

This awareness that the market is a sub-set and an embedded system in both the 'socio-sphere' that in turn is a part of the 'bio-sphere', naturally and self-evident makes the sustainopreneurial team to maximize harmony with life support systems.

Icons of 'Business Activity for Sustainability'

Microentrepreneurship has been a part of the poverty eradication agenda ever since Muhammad Yunus and the Grameen Bank of Bangladesh was focussing 'poverty lending', aimed to support the poor, to provide the means to help themselves out of poverty — *'From Beggar to Businessperson'*. UN recognized the year 2005 as the Year of Microcredit. As a crown on the development starting with Muhammad Yunus first micro-lending from his private pocket 1976 to the Bangla women villagers living outside his University Campus, Muhammad and Grameen Bank in the year 2006, shares the Nobel Peace Prize. When it comes to the two central concepts, sustainability/sustainable development and entrepreneurship; the concept of entrepreneurship gets the strongest cover. It is my claim that the concept of sustainopreneurship primarily should be an extension of the conceptual body related to entrepreneurship to stretch its meaning into and contextualize it in the sustainability domain, rather than the other way around. Also, sustainability covers with some degree of 'development' aspect. When it comes to innovation, it is still relevant to include it in an extended research .The coverage of the innovation concept is more directly aimed towards 'innovation for sustainability' when shallowly mentioned, and is left almost untouched in the literature review. A weakness to innovations, both 'soft and hard', i. e. biased towards two innovation poles; technical and social — are crucial when it comes to 'entrepreneurship and *innovation* for sustainability'. The full chain of social phenomena and interaction flow *invention and innovation with entrepreneurship* for sustainability is a core for deeper understanding of sustainopreneurship, a clear pointer towards prospective future digestion and research.

Conclusion

In the context of entrepreneurship, the success in the process is possible by social change, when taken to the sustainability context. In line with this purposes and the background motives the followings aspects are required as sustainability stability, innovation creativity, entrepreneurship power to act, endurance patience humility joy, inspiration credibility transparency, enabler norm creator awareness, change dialogue respect, agility integrity and realization results proactive. To give a contemporary view of the entrepreneur-as-societal phenomenon. From entrepreneurship, a number of combinations from sources have been classified as: Public entrepreneurship, Therapists entrepreneurship,? Ethnic entrepreneurship,? Artisan entrepreneurship,? Health sector entrepreneurship,? Informal third world entre-preneurship, Ecological entrepreneurship,? NGO entre-preneurship,? Civic entrepreneurship,? Education/university entrepreneurship, City entrepreneurship and? Social entrepreneurship. Further, Sustainability entrepreneurship create the concept *sustainopreneurship by* using of entrepreneurial activity in a *determined action orientation towards solving a sustainability-related problem* with business organising as a means to solve the problem(s) — *'business with a cause'*: To turn business activity from a part of the problem to a part of the solution. The dimension relating to *sustainopreneurship* are:

(a) Seeking, finding and/or creating innovations to solve sustainability-related problems and innovative solutions to the problems related to the sustainability agenda;

(b) Getting solutions to the market through creative organizing;

(c) Adding sustainability value with respect for life support systems. So there is a need to break down the barriers, to sit around in peaceful manner in a circle, to take our collective assets to enhance the sustainability innovations.

References

1. Abrahamsson, A. (2006), Sustainopreneurship—Business with a Cause, in Science for Sustainable Development—Starting Points and Critical Reflections, Uppsala: VHU–Föreningen Vetenskap för Hållbar Utveckling (Swedish Society for Sustainable Development), pp. 21-30.

2. Argyris, C.; Schön, D. (1978), Organizational Learning: A Theory of Action Perspective, Reading, Mass.: Addison Wesley. pp. 23-34.

3. Biggs, M. A. R. (2004) Learning from Experience: Approaches to the Experiential Component of Practice-based Research in Forskning, Reflektion, Utveckling, Stockholm: 2004, pp. 6-21.

4. Blue, J. (2005), Reneuring: Managing for Results, London: Scott Foresman, in Shaper. M. (2005).

5. Bygrave, W. D. (1989), The Entrepreneurship Paradigm: A Philosophical Look at Its Research Methodologies, Entrepreneurship Theory and Practice, Vol. 14 No. (1), pp. 1-26.

6. Gartner, W. B. (1990), What are we Talking About When We Talk About Entrepreneurship, *Journal of Business Venturing*, 5:1, pp. 15-29.

7. Granovetter, M. (1973), The Strength of Weak Ties, *The American Journal of Sociology*, Vol . 78 No. 6, pp. 201-233.

8. Isaak, R (2005), The Making of the Ecopreneur, in Shaper, M. (ed) et al. (2005) Making Ecopreneurs: Developing Sustainable Entrepreneurship Hampshire: Ashgate Publishing Limited, pp. 13-26.

9. Johannisson, B. (1988), Business Formation —A Network Approach, *Scandinavian Journal of Management*,Vol. 4 No. (3/4), pp. 83-89.

10. Lanzara, G.F. (1983), Ephemeral Organizations in Extreme Environments: Emergence, Strategy, Extinction, *Journal of Management Studies*, Vol. 20, No. 1, pp. 71-95.

11. Quinn, J. B. (1971), Next Big Industry: Environmental Improvement, Harvard Business Review , Vol. 49 No. (5), pp. 120-131.

12. Vetenskap för Hållbar Utveckling (Swedish Society for Sustainable Development), pp. 234-244.

Women Entrepreneurship

Progress of the Fairer Sex in India

Dr. Sanjay R. Ajmeri

ABSTRACT

Women Entrepreneur has been recognized during the last couple of decades as an important untapped source of economic growth. The challenges and opportunities provided to the women of digital era are growing rapidly as the jobseekers are turning into job creators. They are flourishing as designers, interior decorators, exporters, publishers, garment manufacturers and still exploring new avenues of economic participation. Indian women business owners are changing the face of businesses of today, both literally and figuratively.

This chapter contains the challenges faced by women entrepreneurs in India, opportunities available to them, and remedial measures to be adopted to promote the entrepreneurship amongst women in India.

Introduction

Women Entrepreneur has been recognized during the last couple of decades as an important untapped source of economic growth. Women Entrepreneurs create new jobs not only for themselves but also for others. They provide society with varied solutions to management, organization and business problems as well as to the exploitation of women entrepreneurial opportunities.

Women owned businesses are highly increasing in the almost all economies of the world. The hidden entrepreneurial potentials of women have gradually been changing with the growing sensitivity to their role and economic status in the society. Skill, knowledge and adaptability in business are the main reasons for women to emerge into business ventures.

The challenges and opportunities provided to the women of digital era are growing rapidly as the job seekers are turning into job creators. They are flourishing as designers, interior decorators, exporters, publishers, garment manufacturers and still exploring new avenues of economic participation. In India, although women constitute the majority of the total population, the entrepreneurial world is still a male dominated one. Women in advanced nations are recognized and are more prominent in the business world.

Concept of Women Entrepreneurship

Women Entrepreneurs may be defined as the women or a group of women who initiate, organize and operate a business enterprise.

Government of India has defined women entrepreneurs as an enterprise owned and controlled by a women having a minimum financial interest of 51 per cent of the capital and giving at least 51 per cent of employment generated in the enterprise to women. Like a male entrepreneurs a women entrepreneur has many functions. They explore the prospects of starting new enterprise; undertake risks; introduction of new innovations; coordination administration and control of business and providing effective leadership in all aspects of business.

Growth of Women Entrepreneurship in India

Women in business are a recent phenomenon in India. India has emerged as the testing ground for budding Indian women entrepreneurs. The progress of the fairer sex in India has been remarkable over the past few decades. By and large they had confide themselves to petty business and tiny cottage industries. A sense towards independent decision-making on their life and career is the motivational factor behind the entrepreneurial urge. In India women are saddled with household chores and domestic responsibilities, and now want to get independence under the influence of these factors. They choose a profession as a challenge and as an urge to do something new or engage themselves in business activities due to family compulsion and the responsibility is thrust upon them. Indian women business owners are changing the face of businesses of today, both literally and figuratively. The dynamic growth and expansion of women-owned businesses is one of the defining trends of the past few decades, and all indications are that it will continue unabated.

During the last few decades, Indian women have entered the field of entrepreneurship in greatly increasing numbers. They have contributed to the global economy and to their surrounding communities with the emergence and growth of their businesses.

Several factors are responsible for increasing the level of female entrepreneurship in India:

- Women enter into entrepreneurial activity because regular employment does not provide them with the flexibility, control or challenge offered by business ownership.
- Evidences show that women do not lack the motivation to enter into business ownership. They are often highly motivated than their male counterparts to overcome the barriers to business start-up.
- Indian women are becoming more empowered today. Legislation is being progressively drafted to offer them more and equal opportunities at various levels.
- Population growth results in a strong positive relationship on entrepreneurial activity. Across genders, the increase in demand and competition for jobs pushes more people into necessary entrepreneurship. For women, in particular, the relatively high involvement in

necessary entrepreneurship indicates that self-employment is used as a way to circumvent institutional and cultural constraints with respect to female employment, as well as a way to provide supplemental family income.

- Auspicious economic conditions favour the participation of women in entrepreneurial activity. The small amount of capital requirement and higher proportion of available bank loans positively correlates the level of female entrepreneurship to economic conditions.
- Increased levels of education have played a crucial role in initiating the process of entrepreneurship among women. It is not only the illiterate that are starting the businesses but those with education and skills are also exploiting profit opportunities.

Characteristics of Women Entrepreneurs in India

Today Indian women have taken rapid strides towards business ownership. Management and interpersonal skills come naturally to women as expert homemakers. The broad classification of women business owners include:

- Women who establish, inherit, or acquire a business.
- Women who start businesses with spouses or business partners but are either at the forefront or behind the scenes.
- Women who start fast-growing or part-time or slow-growing firms.

In comparison to their women counterparts who established their businesses two decades earlier, women who have started their businesses sometime during the past decade are more likely to have:

- a higher level of education, past professional, managerial experience, and executive level experience;
- a greater appetite for capital, both credit and equity;
- a strong motivation for autonomy and achievement;

- a dynamic personality;
- a passion for what they do;
- creativity to innovate and implement;
- independence and self reliance;
- high self confidence;
- willingness and ability to take risks;
- alertness to opportunities;
- ability to marshal resources; and
- ability to respond to market and environment signals.

Indian women are not only educated, talented, confident, assertive, ambitious, career oriented but they also know their minds. Hence, foresight, time management ability, patience, negotiating and budgeting skills of entrepreneurs are integrated in the modern women. The traits of personality of women entrepreneurs are: Risk taker, Proactive, Opportunist, Visionary, Inventor, Tolerance, Desire for independence, Innovator, Ability to bounce back, Flexible, Results oriented, Need for achievement, Internal control, Decisive, Self confident, and Self Motivated.

Ekta Kapoor, Kiran Mazumdar Shaw, Shahnaz Husain, Vimalben M Pawale, Mallika Srinivasan, Naina Lal Kidwai, Sulajja Firodia Motwani, Shobhana Bhartia are some of the successful women entrepreneurs of India.

Challenges of Women Entrepreneurship

Like every sector has its own challenges, the women entrepreneurship is not different. When it comes to having a woman at the helm of a business venture, things do become challenging as there are a lot of socio-cultural biases that need to be dealt with.

- *Lack of an easy access to financing:* Entrepreneurs usually require financial assistance of some kind to launch their ventures — be it a formal bank loan or money from a savings account. Women in developing nations have little access to funds, due to the fact that they are concentrated in poor rural communities with few opportunities to borrow money. The women entrepreneurs are suffering from inadequate financial resources and working capital. The women entrepreneurs lack access to external funds due to their inability to provide tangible security. Very few women have the tangible property in hand.

- *External finance and sex discrimination:* In general, women have lower personal financial assets than men. This means that for a given opportunity and equally capable individual, women must secure additional resources compared to men in order to exploit the opportunity because they control less capital. A question that has developed into its own sub-field in the women's entrepreneurship literature is that women have a harder time getting finance than men for the same business opportunity. The financial institutions are skeptical about the entrepreneurial abilities of women. The bankers consider women loonies as higher risk than men loonies. The bankers put unrealistic and unreasonable securities to get loan to women entrepreneurs.
- *Unawareness about the financial assistance:* Various institutions in the financial sector extend their maximum support in the form of incentives, loans, schemes etc. Even though every woman entrepreneur may not be aware of all the assistance provided by the institutions. So the sincere efforts taken towards women entrepreneurs may not reach the entrepreneurs in rural and backward areas.
- *Lack of role models in entrepreneurship:* There exists a strong connection between the presence of role models and the emergence of entrepreneurs and women as they historically have not been present as entrepreneurs in general lack close role models. Role models are persons that by their attitudes, behaviours and actions establish the desirability and credibility of a choice (in this case becoming an entrepreneur) for an individual.

Furthermore, the influence of role models is gender related. That is, an individual will be more influenced by another individual of the same sex, as one's aspirations and choices tend to be more influenced by persons of the same sex.

- *Lack of experience:* All stages in entrepreneurship are dependent on relevant experience, from the identification of opportunities to the execution of running a business. Depending on their levels of human capital, individuals differ in their ability to discover and exploit opportunities. People have access to different information and process it differently depending on idiosyncratic knowledge and preferences. Therefore, the ability to discover and exploit opportunities depends largely on past education and work experience.
- *Lack of confidence:* In general, women lack confidence in their strength and competence. The family members and the society are reluctant to stand beside their entrepreneurial growth.
- *Gender Discrimination and Stereotyping:* Challenges for women begin in childhood. Young girls may be brought up to believe that they are only suited for certain professions or, in some cases, only to serve as wives and mothers. Gender lines are drawn early, and exclusions for women continue throughout adulthood. These constant messages may lead to a false belief that women do not belong in the high-powered corporate world.
- *The greatest deterrent to women entrepreneurs is that they are women*. A kind of patriarchal – male dominant social order is the building block to them in their way towards business success. Male members think it a big risk financing the ventures run by women. The male - female competition is another factor, which develop hurdles to women entrepreneurs in the business management process. Despite the fact that women entrepreneurs are good in keeping their service prompt and delivery in time, due to lack of organisational skills compared to

male entrepreneurs women have to face constraints from competition. The confidence to travel across day and night and even different regions and states are less found in women compared to male entrepreneurs. This shows the low level freedom of expression and freedom of mobility of the women entrepreneurs.

- *Family obligations:* Women's family obligations also bar them from becoming successful entrepreneurs. Having primary responsibility for children, home and older dependent family members, few women can devote all their time and energies to their business. The financial institutions discourage women entrepreneurs on the belief that they can at any time leave their business and become housewives again. The result is that they are forced to rely on their own savings, and loan from relatives and family friends.
- *Socio-cultural barriers/Dual career/Family pressures:* Women's family and personal obligations are sometimes a great barrier for succeeding in business career. Only few women are able to manage both home and business efficiently, devoting enough time to perform all their responsibilities in priority. Indian women give more emphasis to family ties and relationships. Married women have to make a fine balance between business and home. More over the business success is depends on the support the family members extended to women in the business process and management. The interest of the family members is a determinant factor in the realization of women-folk business aspirations.
- *Knowledge in Business Administration:* Women must be educated and trained constantly to acquire the skills and knowledge in all the functional areas of business management. This can facilitate women to excel in decision-making process and develop a good business network. The argument is that women entrepreneurs have low-level management skills. They have to depend

on office staffs and intermediaries, to get things done, especially, the marketing and sales side of business. Here there is more probability for business fallacies like the intermediaries take major part of the surplus or profit. Marketing means mobility and confidence in dealing with the external world, both of which women have been discouraged from developing by social conditioning. Even when they are otherwise in control of an enterprise, they often depend on males of the family in this area.

- *Market-oriented risks:* Stiff competition in the market and lack of mobility of women make the dependence of women entrepreneurs on middleman indispensable. Many business women find it difficult to capture the market and make their products popular. They are not fully aware of the changing market conditions and hence can effectively utilize the services of media and internet.
- *Motivational factors:* Self motivation can be realized through a mind set for a successful business, attitude to take up risk and behavior towards the business society by shouldering the social responsibilities. Other factors are family support, Government policies, financial assistance from public and private institutions and also the environment suitable for women to establish business units. Achievement motivation of the women-folk found less compared to male members. The low level of education and confidence leads to low level achievement and advancement motivation among women-folk to engage in business operations and running a business concern.
- *Identifying the available resources:* Women are hesitant to find out the access to cater their needs in the financial and marketing areas. In spite of the mushrooming growth of associations, institutions, and the schemes from the government side, women are not enterprising and dynamic to optimize the resources in the form of reserves, assets, and mankind or business volunteers. Knowledge

of alternative source of raw materials availability and high negotiation skills are the basic requirement to run a business. Getting the raw materials from different source with discount prices is the factor that determines the profit margin. Lack of knowledge of availability of the raw materials and low-level negotiation and bargaining skills are the factors, which affect women entrepreneur's business adventures.

- *Unexposed to the training programmes:* Training programs and workshops for every type of entrepreneur is available through the social and welfare associations, based on duration, skill and the purpose of the training program. Such programs are really useful to new, rural and young entrepreneurs who want to set up a small and medium scale unit on their own.
- *Lack of technical knowledge:* Knowledge of latest technological changes, know-how, and education level of the person are significant factor that affect business. The literacy rate of women in India is found at low level compared to male population. Many women in developing nations lack the education needed to spur successful entrepreneurship. They are ignorant of new technologies or unskilled in their use, and often unable to do research and gain the necessary training. Although great advances are being made in technology, many women's illiteracy, structural difficulties, and lack of access to technical training prevent the technology from being beneficial or even available to females.
- *Low-level risk taking attitude:* Another factor affecting women folk decision to get into business is Low-level risk taking attitude. Low-level education provides low-level self-confidence and self-reliance to the women-folk to engage in business, which is continuous risk taking and strategic decision-making profession. Investing money, maintaining the operations and ploughing back money for surplus generation requires high risk taking attitude, courage and confidence. Though the risk

tolerance ability of the women-folk in day-to-day life is high compared to male members, while in business it is found opposite to that.

- *Lack of wealth:* A prerequisite for starting a firm is to have capital in terms of financial assets and in terms of relevant knowledge assets. Women's position in society has led to a lack of assets in both these aspects. The constraints of family obligations make it harder for women to take on work on a full time basis and to engage in a career. This in turn decreases the range of possible work opportunities for women, leading to jobs in lower paid sectors. Being a part-time worker with low pay is not a good basis for creating personal wealth.

In a nutshell, the specific obstacles to Women Entrepreneur are: type of education, lack of role models in Women Entrepreneurship, gendering of Women Entrepreneurship, weak social status, competing demands on time and access to finance. Hence ,Women Entrepreneur must be examined both at the individual level (*i.e.* the choice of becoming self-employed) and at the firm level (the performance of women owned and managed firms) in order to fully understand the differences between men and Women Entrepreneur, since they play an effective role for contributing a mite to the economic development of the country.

Opportunities

When it comes to tapping the business verticals, the sky is the limit. The basics of this are women entrepreneurs need creativity and entrepreneurial skills, which can be fine tuned with time and experience. Textile, food processing, block printing or IT business are some popular SME domains for women. The additional business opportunities that are recently approaching for women entrepreneurs are: Eco-friendly technology, Bio-technology, IT enabled enterprises, Event Management, Tourism industry, Telecommunication, Plastic materials, Vermiculture, Mineral water, Sericulture, Floriculture, Herbal and health care and Food, fruits and vegetable processing.

Remedial Measures

Empowering women entrepreneurs is essential for achieving the goals of sustainable development and the bottlenecks hindering their growth must be eradicated to entitle full participation in the business. Apart from training programs, Newsletters, mentoring, trade fairs and exhibitions also can be a source for entrepreneurial development. As a result, the desired outcomes of the business are quickly achieved and more of remunerative business opportunities are found.

Promoting entrepreneurship for women will require an even greater reversal of traditional attitudes than the mere creation of jobs for women would. This does not mean that we should wait for societal change to take place first. But it does imply that the programme should go beyond subsidies and credit allocation to attitudinal changes, group formation, training and other support services.

In order to realize the benefits of policy changes it is important to incorporate a Women Entrepreneurial dimension in considering all SMEs and growth policies (*e.g.* meeting Women financing needs at all stages of the business continuum; take-up of business development and support services; access to corporate, government and international markets; technology access and utilization; R & D and innovation; etc.). Moreover this means periodically evaluating the impact of these measures on the success of women-owned businesses and exchanging good models and best practices, through cooperation with leading international organizations such as the OECD, European Union, APEC, UNCTAD and the ILO, in order to continually improve policies and Proposals.

It is important to create the right environment for entrepreneurs to face the challenges and to get success in their business. Thus, the areas which are to be focussed are:

- Create the conducive environment for success;
- Ensure that they have access to the right skill;
- Ensure that they have access to the smart capital, enable networking and exchange;

Some of the suggestive measures are:

Better qualitative information and quantitative data and statistics are required to profile Women Entrepreneurs (demographic information, barriers to start-up and growth). This would also assist in promoting awareness of the role of Women Entrepreneurs in the economy.

Promote the development of Women Entrepreneur networks. It is observed that Women Entrepreneur networks are major sources of knowledge about Women Entrepreneur and they are increasingly recognized as a valuable tool for its development and promotion. Policy makers must foster the networking of associations and encourage co-operation and partnerships among national and international networks and facilitate Women Entrepreneurial endeavors by women in the economy. These are major sources of knowledge about Women Entrepreneur and valuable tools for its development and promotion. Co-operation and partnerships between national and international networks can facilitate Women Entrepreneurial endeavors by women in a global economy.

The creation of government offices of Women business ownership is one way to facilitate this. Such offices could have programmed responsibilities such as providing Women business centres, organizing information seminars and meetings and/or providing web-based information to those wanting to start and grow a business.

Incorporate a Women Entrepreneurial dimension in the formation of all SME-related policies. This can be done by ensuring that the impact on Women Entrepreneur is taken into account at the design stage. Periodically evaluate the impact of any SME-related policies on the success of women-owned businesses and the extent to which such businesses take advantage of them.

Improve the factual and analytical underpinnings of our understanding of the role of Women Entrepreneurs in the economy. This requires strengthening the statistical basis for carrying out gender-related cross-country comparative analyses and longitudinal studies of the impact of important developments and policies, especially over time. Policy measures to support women's entrepreneurship can go along some different lines. Policy makers can:

- Increase the ability of women to participate in the labour force by ensuring the availability of affordable child care and equal treatment in the work place. More generally, improving the position of women in society and promoting entrepreneurship generally will have benefits in terms of women's entrepreneurship.
- Listen to the voice of women entrepreneurs. The creation of government offices of women's business ownership is one way to facilitate this. Such offices could have programme responsibilities such as providing women's business centres, organising information seminars and meetings and/or providing web-based information to women who are already entrepreneurs and who have important insights into the changes needed to improve women's entrepreneurship.
- Incorporate a women's entrepreneurial dimension in the formation of all SME-related policies. This can be done by ensuring that the impact on women's entrepreneurship is taken into account at the design stage.
- Promote the development of women entrepreneur networks. These are major sources of knowledge about women's entrepreneurship and valuable tools for its development and promotion. Co-operation and partnerships between national and international networks can facilitate entrepreneurial endeavours by women in a global economy.
- Periodically evaluate the impact of any SME-related policies on the success of women-owned businesses and the extent to which such businesses take advantage of them. The objective should be to identify ways to improve the effectiveness of those that should be retained. Good practices that are identified in this way should be disseminated and shared internationally.

- Improve the factual and analytical underpinnings of our understanding of the role of women entrepreneurs in the economy. This requires strengthening the statistical basis for carrying out gender-related cross-country comparative analyses and longitudinal studies of the impact of important developments and policies, especially over time.

References

1. Jose P., Ajith Kumar and Paul T.M., (1994), *Entrepreneurship Development*, Himalaya Publishing.
2. Dr. C. B. Gupta and Dr. N. P. Srinivasan, *Entrepreneurship Development in India*, Sultan Chand & Sons.
3. Vasant Desai, Dynamics of Entrepreneurial Development and Management, Himalaya Publishing House.
4. E. Gordon and E. Natarajan, *Entrepreneuship Development*, Himalaya Publishing House.
5. Surekha Panandikar, "Women Entrepreneurs: Problems and Potential", *Economics Times*, Dec. 26, 1985.
6. Sayanti Banerjee, Smart Ma'am Entrepreneurs, *Economics Times*, Sept. 25, 2008.
7. A. Vaarmathi, Challenges to Entrepreneurial Development of Women in India, *The Economic Challenger*, No. 12, Issue 47, April-June 2010.
8. Renuka V. (2001), Opportunities and Challenges for Women in Business, India Together, Online Report, Civil Society Information Exchange Pvt. Ltd.
9. Moinak Mitra, What Ails Woman Entrepreneurship in India?, *Economic Times*, 20 Jun, 2008.

Women Empowerment and Microfinance in India
Issues and Challenges

Dr. Rais Ahmad,
Mr. Ashraf Imam

ABSTRACT

In developing countries like India women's entrepreneurs face a comparative disadvantage for operating high-productivity activities, due to the frequency of patriarchal forms of business regulations. If a microfinance institution (MFIs) wants to succeed then it should enhancing women empowerment, increased access to credit must enable women entrepreneurs to tap into the range of high-productivity activities. So when the costs of legality are too high in developing countries and the informal economy becomes the only affordable venue for operating a business venture. This chapter shows that access to microfinance services not sufficient for women empowerment and basics of microfinance and its issues and challenges.

Keywords: Microfinance, Women Entrepreneurship, MFIs, Empowerment

Introduction

Empowerment is the one of the key factors in determining the success of development is the status and position of women in the society. We should focus especially on empowering women as they hold the key to long-lasting social change in communities. Empowering women must be an integrated approach, a cause that requires continued attention. There is need to augment our efforts for empowering women and enhance their progress. It is our moral, social and constitutional responsibility to ensure their progress by providing them with equal rights and opportunities. Today women with their grace and elegance have conquered the whole world. They with their hard work and sincerity have excelled in each and every profession. Women are considered to be more honest, meticulous, and efficient and hence more and more companies prefer hiring women for better performance and result. It is a known fact that many companies prefer to have women candidates for certain jobs. Some websites like http://naukriforwomen.com aspires to help companies reach suitable women candidates for their job vacancies. This is a good initiative to bring women empowerment in India.

Empowerment refers to increasing the spiritual, political, social, or economic strength of individuals and communities. It often involves the empowered developing confidence in their own capacities and the empowerment of women, also called gender empowerment, has become a significant topic of discussion in regards to development and economics. Entire nations, businesses, communities, and groups can benefit from the implementation of programmes and policies that adopt the notion of women empowerment.

Empowerment as having a number of qualities, as follows:

- Having decision-making power;
- Having access to information and resources;
- Having a range of options from which to make choices (not just yes/no, either/or);

- Assertiveness;
- A feeling that the individual can make a difference (being hopeful);
- Learning to think critically; learning the conditioning; seeing things differently;
- Learning to redefine who we are (speaking in our own voice);
- Learning to redefine what we can do;
- Learning to redefine our relationships to institutionalized power;
- Learning about and expressing anger;
- Not feeling alone; feeling part of a group;
- Understanding that people have rights;
- Effecting change in one's life and one's community;
- Learning skills (*e.g.*, communication) that the individual defines as important;
- Changing others' perceptions of one's competency and capacity to act;
- Coming out of the closet;
- Growth and change that is never ending and self-initiated;
- Increasing one's positive self-image and overcoming stigma.

Women Empowerment and Microfinance in India: A Conceptual Framework

Microfinance is promising as a powerful instrument for poverty alleviation in India. In India, Microfinance scene is dominated by Self Help Group (SHGs)-Bank Linkage Programme as a cost effective mechanism for providing financial services to the unreachable poor peoples which has been successful not only in meeting financial needs of the rural peoples and women but also reinforce collective self help capacities of the poor leading to their empowerment.

Swift progress in SHG formation has now turned into an empowerment movement among women across the country. Economic empowerment results in women's ability to influence or make decision, increased self confidence, better status and role in household etc. Micro finance is necessary to overcome exploitation, create confidence for economic self reliance of the rural poor, particularly among rural women who are mostly invisible in the social structure. Micro finance has received extensive recognition as a strategy for economic empowerment of women.

Women Empowerment

Women Empowerment refers to increasing the spiritual, political, social or economic strength of Women. It often involves the empowered developing confidence in their own capacities. Women empowerment is probably the totality of the following or similar given above capabilities:

- Having decision-making power of their own;
- Having access to information and resources for taking proper decision;
- Having a range of options from which you can make choices (not just yes/no, either/or);
- Ability to exercise assertiveness in collective decision making;
- Having positive thinking on the ability to make change;
- Ability to learn skills for improving one's personal or group power;
- Ability to change others' perceptions by democratic means;
- Involving in the growth process and changes that is never ending and self-initiated;
- Increasing one's positive self-image and overcoming stigma.

Women in India now participate in all activities such as education, politics, media, art and culture, service sectors, science and technology, etc. The Constitution of India guarantees to all Indian women equality (Article 14), no discrimination by the State (Article 15(1), equality of opportunity (Article 16), equal pay for equal work (Article 39(d)). In addition, it allows special provisions to be made by the State in favour of women and children (Article 15(3), renounces practices derogatory to the dignity of women (Article 51(A) (e)), and also allows for provisions to be made by the State for securing just and humane conditions of work and for maternity relief. (Article 42). The feminist activism in India picked up momentum during later 1970s. One of the first national level issues that brought the women's groups together was the Mathura rape case. The acquittal of policemen accused of raping a young girl Mathura in a police station, led to a wide-scale protests in 1979–1980. In 1990s, grants from foreign donor agencies enabled the formation of new women-oriented NGOs. Self-help groups and NGOs such as Self Employed Women's Association (SEWA) have played a major role in women's rights in India. Many women have emerged as leaders of local movements. For example, Medha Patkar of the Narmada Bachao Andolan. The Government of India declared 2001 as the Year of Women's Empowerment (Swashakti). The National Policy for the Empowerment of Women was passed in 2001.

Microfinance in India

Micro-finance addressing issues related to poverty alleviation, financial support to micro entrepreneurs, gender development etc. There is, however, no statutory definition of micro finance. The taskforce on supportive policy and Regulatory Framework for Microfinance has defined microfinance as "Provision of thrift, credit and other financial services and products of very small amounts to the poor in rural, semi-urban or urban areas for enabling them to raise their income levels and improve living standards". The term 'Micro' literally means 'small'. But the task force has not defined any amount. However as per Micro Credit Special Cell of the Reserve Bank of India, the borrowed amounts up to the limit of Rs. 25000/- could be considered as micro credit products and this amount could be gradually increased up to Rs.40000/- over a period of time which roughly equals to $500 — a standard for South Asia as per international perceptions. The term micro finance, sometimes is used interchangeably with the term micro credit. However while micro credit refers to purveyance of loans in small quantities, the term microfinance has a broader meaning covering in its ambit other financial services like saving, insurance etc. as well. The mantra 'Microfinance' is banking through groups. The essential features of the approach are to provide financial services through the groups of individuals, formed either in joint liability or co-obligation mode. The other dimensions of the microfinance approach are:

- Savings/Thrift precedes credit
- Credit is linked with savings/thrift
- Lack of subsidies
- Group plays an important role in credit appraisal, monitoring and recovery.

Basically Groups Can Be of Two Types

Self Help Groups (SHGs): The group in this case does financial intermediation on behalf of the formal institution. This is the predominant model followed in India.

Grameen Groups: In this model, financial assistance is provided to the individual in a group by the formal institution on the strength of group's assurance. In other words, individual loans are provided on the strength of joint liability/ co obligation. This microfinance model was initiated by Bangladesh Grameen Bank and is being used by some of the Micro Finance Institutions (MFIs) in our country.

Microfinance is the provision of financial services to low-income clients or solidarity lending groups including consumers and the self-employed, who traditionally lack access to banking and related services. More broadly, it is a movement whose object is "a world in which as many poor and near-poor households as possible have permanent access to an appropriate range of high quality financial services, including not just credit but also savings, insurance, and fund transfers.

Microfinance Companies in India

Microfinance companies are the financial institutions that offer small-scale financial services in both the forms – credit and savings, especially to the poor in rural, semi-urban and urban areas. These financial services are meant to help them in undertaking economic activities, mitigating vulnerabilities to income shocks, smoothening consumption, increasing savings and supporting self-empowerment. There are a number of microfinance companies in India, which play some pivotal roles to the development of India.

India's microfinance sector is fragmented with more than 3000 microfinance companies (MFIs), NGOs and NGO-MFIs. The top 10 microfinance companies in India are estimated to account for almost 74 per cent of the total loans outstanding. It can be added here that the total loan outstanding of Indian microfinance sector lies between Rs. 160-175 billion. As on March 31, 2009, almost 17 Indian microfinance companies have more Rs. 1 million outstanding loans. Following are the top 10 Microfinance companies in India:

SKS Microfinance Ltd (SKSMPL)

Spandana Sphoorty Financial Ltd (SSFL)

Share Microfinance Limited (SML)

Asmitha Microfinance Ltd (AML)

Shri Kshetra Dharmasthala Rural Development Project (SKDRDP)

Bhartiya Samruddhi Finance Limited (BSFL)

Bandhan

Cashpor Micro Credit (CMC)

Grama Vidiyal Micro Finance Pvt Ltd (GVMFL)

Grameen Financial Services Pvt Ltd (GFSPL)

Microfinance is being increasingly recognized as a sustainable solution for developmental interventions. In fact, the success of some innovative experiments to alleviate poverty in countries has proved that small credit given to the poor can effectively increase their income-level through entrepreneurship and skill support development. In addition to this, it has also been noted that catalyst agencies such as NGOs also benefit from this new practices of sustainable development. NGOs are not seen merely as passing on the donor agenda to the community in a micro-insurance project; they are, in fact, looked upon as professionals change makers, actively delivering services to the poor and benefiting from them. The benefit not only motivates them for extending the services, but also improves their own sustainability. There are many examples like SPANDANA in India and Grameen Bank in Bangladesh, which have not only succeeded in providing innovative and sustainable services to the poor, but also helped themselves in creating sustainable service-oriented outlets. NGOs, who have gained profits by providing microcredit services to the poor, have managed to build resources for their own organization in such a manner that they are now funding their own developmental projects, without being dependent upon donor agencies. Microfinance can evolve further into new business directions for the NGOs. The end-result of all microfinance operations is the establishment of a strong and sustainable community-based organization. Since women's empowerment is the key to socio-economic development of the community; bringing women into the mainstream of national development has been a major concern of government. The ministry of rural development has special components for women in its programmes. Funds are earmarked as 'Women's component' to ensure flow of adequate resources for the same. Besides Swarnagayanti Grameen Swarazgar Yojona (SGSY), Ministry of Rural Development is implementing other scheme having women's component .They are the Indira Awas Yojona (IAJ), National Social Assistance Programme (NSAP), Restructured Rural Sanitation Programme, Accelerated Rural Water Supply programme (ARWSP) the (erstwhile) Integrated Rural Development Programme (IRDP), the (erstwhile) Development of Women and Children in Rural Areas (DWCRA) and the Jowahar Rozgar Yojana (JRY).

Microfinance: Empowering Women in India

Microcredit also offers a way to provide empowerment for women. Governments, organizations, and individuals have caught hold of the lure of microfinance. They hope that lending money and credit allows women to function in business and society, which in turn empowers them to do more in their communities. One of the primary goals in the foundation of microfinance was women empowerment. Loans with low interest rates are given to women in developing communities in hopes that they can start a small business and provide for her family. Empowerment of women in India through microfinance is now a proven strategy for their development. The Microcredit Summit Campaign reports (http://www.microcreditsummit.org/) that 14.2 million of the world's poorest women now have access to financial services which accounting for nearly 74 per cent of the 19.3 million poorest served by microfinance. Further, microfinance institutions often lack women in governance, management and operations, meaning that woman's voices and perspectives are not always incorporated into the design and implementation of products and services. There are good reasons to aim women empowerment. Gender equality turns out to be good for everybody. The World Bank reports that societies that discriminate on the basis of gender have greater poverty, slower economic growth, weaker governance, and a lower standard of living. Women are poorer and more disadvantaged than men. Several Studies shows that men typically contribute more than fifty per cent of their salaries to the collective household fund, whereas women tend to keep nothing back for themselves and women contribute decisively to the well-being of their families.

Investing in women brings about a multiplier effect. Finally, every microfinance institution has stories of women who not only are better off economically as a result of access to financial services, but who are empowered as well. Simply getting cash into the hands of women (by way of working capital) can lead to increased self-esteem, control and empowerment by helping them achieve greater economic independence and security, which in turn gives them the chance to contribute financially to their households and societies.

Empowerment is about transform, option and authority. It is a process of change by which individuals and groups with little or no power gain the power and ability to make choices that affect their lives. The ability of a woman to transform her life through access to financial services depends on many factors some of them linked to her individual situation and abilities, and others dependent upon her environment and the status of women as a group.

Microfinance programmes can have implausible impact on the empowerment process if their products and services take these circumstances into account. While many microfinance institutions in India seek to empower women as an inherent or open goal, others believe they cannot afford to focus on empowerment because it is incompatible with financial sustainability or because it detracts from the core business of providing financial services. Several researches also show abundant evidence of efficient, sustainable microfinance institutions whose programmes are intentionally empowering. In some cases, it is through a commitment to excellent customer service, including people at all levels of the organization treating clients with respect. In other cases, soft services such as health education, literacy training or business training can be packaged with financial services in a way that creates economies of scope and powerful synergies, and can even help reduce client exit and arrears.

Women Empowerment Through Microfinance Why?

- Increased Self-Confidence and Self-esteem in women and showing more participation in Decision-making.

- Brazenness and think critically; learning the conditioning; seeing things differently.
- Understanding effecting change in one's life and one's community.
- Learning skills (*e.g.*, communication) that the individual defines as important.
- Changing others' perceptions of one's competency and capacity to act.
- Growth and change that is never ending and self-initiated.

Women clients have also experienced improved status and gender relations in the home and women's financial contributions helped them earn greater respect from their husbands and children, negotiate husbands' help with housework, and avoid family clashes over money. Several studies show that women perceive more respect from their societies than they did before joining a microfinance programme. They also show women taking greater roles in giving advice within the community, organizing for social change, and participating in community meetings in part because they are now able to contribute financially to community needs and activities. But overall there is negative impacts and limitations also to empowerment of women. A number of studies show an increase in women's workloads as they expand their businesses and participate in microfinance meetings. Some women have reported ill health and overtiredness due to work-load from both sides (business and family).

There is cost-effective matter is also concern in bringing about women's empowerment like number of programmatic practices that are worth looking at including business training, investing in women's general education and literacy, providing guidance in balancing family and work responsibilities, providing a forum for dialogue on social and political issues, such as women' rights and community problems, giving women experience in decision-making, and promoting women's ownership, control and participatory governance in their microfinance programmes. Microfinance programs have been very successful in reaching women. This gives microfinance institutions an extraordinary opportunity to act intentionally to empower women especially unreachable poor rural women and to minimize the potentially negative impacts by experiencing from some women entrepneurs. Empowering women puts the spotlight on education and employment which are an essential element to sustainable development.

Issues and Challenges of Women Empowerment Through Microfinance

Many of the obstructions to women empowerment lie ingrained into the cultures of certain nations and societies. Many women feel these pressures, while others have become acclimatize to being treated inferior to men. Even if men, legislators, NGOs, etc. are aware of the benefits women empowerment and participation can have, many are scared of disrupting the status quo and continue to let societal norms get in the way of development. Empowerment of women is closely related to formal and informal sources of education. Women's education is extremely important intrinsically as it is their human right and required for the flourishing of many of their capacities. Elements that contribute to make more difficult for women empowerment through micro-finance:

- Insufficient knowledge of the market and potentiality, therefore making the choice of business difficult.
- Poor accounting of business transactions.
- Employment of family members or relatives which increases social pressure to contribute to benefits.
- Setting prices illogically.
- Lack of sufficient capital.
- High interest rates.
- Inventory and inflation accounting management is never in a absolute figures.

- Credit policies that can gradually ruin their business (many customers cannot pay cash; on the other hand, suppliers are very harsh towards women).
- Gender inequalities in access to other resources for investment.
- Responsibility for household subsistence expenditure.
- Lack of time because of unpaid domestic work.
- Low levels of mobility or doesn't have frequent travelling ability.
- Credit (*i.e.* debt) may lead to severe impoverishment, abandonment and put serious strains on networks with other women.
- Pressure to save may mean women forgoing their own necessary consumption.
- Programmes based on group lending, and time consuming income generating activities without reduction of traditional responsibilities increase women's work and time burden.
- Lack of economic empowerment for better survival in market: Micro finance assists women to perform traditional roles better and women thus remain trapped in low productivity sectors, not moving from the group of survival enterprises to micro-enterprises.
- Men withdrawing their contributions to certain types of household expenditures which lead to over-burden to women.

Conclusion and Suggestions

Empowerment can be viewed as a means of creating a social environment in which one can take decisions and make choice either individually or collectively for social transformation. It strength innate ability by way of acquiring knowledge power and experience. Numerous traditional and informal system of credit that was already in existence before micro finance came into vogue. Viability of micro finance needs to be understood from a dimension that is far broader- in looking at its long-term aspects too very little attention has been given to empowerment questions or ways in which both empowerment and sustainability aims may be accommodated. Failure to take into account impact on income also has potentially adverse implications for both repayment and outreach, and hence also for financial sustainability. An effort is made here to present some of these aspects to complete the picture. A conclusion that emerges from this account is that micro finance can contribute to solving the problems of inadequate housing and urban services as an integral part of poverty alleviation programmes. The challenge lies in finding the level of flexibility in the credit instrument that could make it match the multiple credit requirements of the low income borrower without imposing unbearably high cost of monitoring its end use upon the lenders. A promising solution is to provide multipurpose lone or composite credit for income generation, housing improvement and consumption support. Consumption loan is found to be especially important during the gestation period between commencing a new economic activity and deriving positive income. Careful research on demand for financing and savings behaviour of the potential borrowers and their participation in determine the mixes of multi-purpose loans are essential in making the concept work. Incorporate programmatic elements such as training or leadership opportunities that contribute to women's empowerment and tracking should be there for empowerment benefits along with institutional financial performance and economic impact indicators. Bring women and women's perspectives into the governance, management, and implementation of microfinance programmes. Government should more supportive and adopt holistic approaches to microfinance as part of an on-going commitment to innovation, research, and development and also conduct and support action research on best practices in empowering women like promoting women in leadership in the MFIs they support. However we should ensured a long-term strategic process in the micro-finance sector for continues to move forward in relation to gender equality and women's empowerment. It is clear that gender strategies in micro finance need to look beyond just increasing women's access to savings and credit and organizing self help groups to look strategically at how programmes can actively promote gender equality and women's empowerment. Moreover the focus should be on developing a diversified micro finance sector where different type of organizations, NGO, MFIs and formal sector banks all should have gender policies adapted to the needs of their particular target groups/institutional roles and capacities and collaborate and work together to make a significant contribution to gender equality and pro-poor development.

References

1. Bardhan, K. and S. Klasen (1999), "UNDP's Gender-related Indices: A Critical Review", World Development, Vol. 27, No. 6.
2. Bardhan, K. and S. Klasen (2000), "On UNDP's Revisions to the Gender-related Development Index", *Journal of Human Development*.
3. Barkat, A. (2008), "Women Empowerment: A Key to Human Development, http://www.goodgovernance.org visited on 10th December 2010 at 6:30 pm.
4. Beteta, K.C. (2006), "What is Missing in Measures of Women's Empowerment?", *Journal of Human Development and Capabilities*, Vol. 7.
5. Bidisha Mahanta, (2008), Women Empowerment in Assam—A Human Development Approach (http://www.pnayak.webs.com/misc_files/mphil _ synopsis _ women _empowerment.pdf)
6. Dijkstra, G. (2002), "Revisiting UNDP's GDI and GEM: Towards an Alternative", Social Indicator Research, Vol. 57, No. 3.
7. Dijkstra, G. (2006), "Towards a Fresh Start in Measuring Gender Equality: A Contribution to the Debate", *Journal of Human Development*, Vol. 7.
8. Government of Assam (2003), "Women: Striving in an Unequal World" in Assam Human Development Report, 2003. http://planassam.org/report/hdr 2003/HDR. html.
9. IFUW (2001): "Empowering Women". <http://www.ifuw.org/saap2001/empowerment.htm.

10. Kishor, S. and K. Gupta (2004), "Women's Empowerment in India and Its States: Evidence from the NFHS", *Economic and Political Weekly*, Vol.XXXIX, No.7.

11. Klasen, S. (2006), "UNDP's Gender-related Measures: Some Conceptual Problems and Possible Solutions", *Journal of Human Development*, Vol.7.

12. Klasen, S. and D. Schüler (2009), "Reforming the Gender-related Development Index (GDI) and the Gender Empowerment Measure (GEM): Some Specific Proposals". http://www2.vwl.wiso.unigoettingen.de/ibero/papers/DB186.pdf.

13. Malhotra, A., S.R. Schuler and C. Boender (2002), "Measuring Women's Empowerment as a Variable in International Development" Unpublished Paper for the World Bank. www.unicef.org/pubsgen/humanrights-children/index.html.

14. Parasar, S. (2004), "A Multidimensional Approach to Women's Empowerment and its Links to the Nutritional Status and Immunization of Children in India". http://www.allacademic.com/meta/p109193index.html.

15. Pillarisetti and Gillivray (1998), "Human Development and Gender Empowerment: Methodological and Measurement Issue" Development Policy Review, Vol. 16.

16. Ranis, G. and F. Stewart (2005), "Dynamic Links Between the Economy and Human Development", *DESA Working Paper No. 8*. http://www.un.org/esa/desa/papers.

17. Shariff, Abusaleh (2009), "Gender Empowerment in India: Concepts and Measurement". http://salehshariff.blogspot.com/2009/09/genderempowerment-in-india-concepts.html.

18. Shields, Lourene E. (1995): "Women's Experiences of the Meaning of Empowerment", Qualitative Health Research, Vol. 5, No.1.

19. UNESCO (1993), Violence Against Women—Reports from India and the Republic of Korea, Social and Human Sciences in Asia and the Pacific, RUSHAP Series of Monographs and Occasional Papers 37, Bangkok. http://unesdoc.unesco.org/images/0009/000966/096629eo.pdf.

Other Related Links

Women Empowerment definition is available at http://wiki.answers.com/Q/Define _ women _ empowerment # ixzz 17 iws EZx0.

http://www.genfinance.info/1Empowerment.htm

Microfinance is available at

http://www.microfinancegateway.org/p/site/m/template.rc/1.26.9183/#1.26.9/83/#1

A Reflection on Women Entrepreneurship

With Special Reference to North Eastern Region of India

Prof. Sanjay Kanti Das

ABSTRACT

Women are to be considered as equal partners in the process of development. But, because of centuries of exploitation and subjugation, Indian women have remained at the receiving end. Women in India have been the neglected lot. They have not been actively involved in the mainstream of development even though they represent equal proportion of the population and labour force. The emergence of women entrepreneurs and their contribution to the national economy is quite visible in India. The number of women entrepreneurs has grown over a period of time, especially in the 1990s.

This chapter aims to study the status of Indian women and most particularly North Eastern region of India in the entrepreneurial world. Efforts are made to reflect the growing trend of women entrepreneurs, their problems and the developmental schemes of the Government of India in this connection. Comparative analysis is also made about the male and female participation in establishing SSI and micro enterprises in the NER and also in the country.

Introduction

Women are to be considered as equal partners in the process of development. But, because of centuries of exploitation and subjugation, Indian women have remained at the receiving end. Women in India have been the neglected lot. They have not been actively involved in the mainstream of development even though they represent equal proportion of the population and labour force. Primarily women are the means of survival of their families, but are generally unrecognized and undervalued, being placed at the bottom of the pile. No country can achieve its potential without adequately investing in and developing the capabilities of women.

A country, which is rich in entrepreneurship, can attain economic augmentation. The entrepreneurs organize the economic ventures for producing goods and services at lower cost with objects of maximization of new employment and setting up new business (Nazar 2005[1]). It is matter of firm belief that the economic development and social progress of women is the key to emancipation of women in its real sense. Women as entrepreneurs have become an important part of national development planning and strategies (Tuladhar 1996[2]). The entrepreneurship shows the path to women independence and in turn satisfies the needs and aspirations for better living standard. In recent years, women have shown an inclination toward taking self oriented jobs and professions with their family support, financial assistance and industrial guidance.

The emergence of women entrepreneurs and their contribution to the national economy is quite visible in India. The number of women entrepreneurs has grown over a period of time, especially in the 1990s. Women's entrepreneurship needs to be studied separately for two main reasons. The first reason is that women's entrepreneurship has been recognized during the last decade as an important untapped source of economic growth. Women entrepreneurs create new jobs for themselves and others and also by being different. They also provide the society with different solutions to management, organisation and business problems as well as to the exploitation of entrepreneurial opportunities. The second reason is that the topic of women in entrepreneurship has been largely neglected both in society in general and in the social sciences. Not only have women lower participation rates in entrepreneurship than men but they also generally choose to start and manage firms in different industries than men tend to do.

The government has an important catalytic role in helping rural population mobilize their own entrepreneurship. An appropriate role of government agencies is therefore to create an enabling environment allowing rural SHGs to grow and perform their functions more effectively to the extent that they become independent, some such groups are unable to function effectively because of lack of professionalism, technical competence and entrepreneurial skills. The government thus also has an important capacity building role so that the SHGs develop into self-reliant organizations over time.[3]

Concept of Women Entrepreneurs

Women Entrepreneurs are the women or a group of women who initiate, organize and operate a business enterprise. The Government of India notes women entrepreneurs as "an enterprise owned and controlled by women saving a minimum financial interest of 51 per cent of the capital and giving at least 51 per cent of the employment generated in the enterprise to women". The participation of women in SSI sector has been identified in three different roles. Some women were owners of enterprises, some were managers of enterprises and some were employees. With regard to ownership, an SSI or a SSSBE managed by one or more women entrepreneurs in proprietary concerns, or in which she/they individually or jointly have a share capital of not less than 51 per cent as partners/share holders/Directors of Private Limited Company/Members of Co-operative Society is called a 'Woman enterprise'.

Women Entrepreneurs in India

Indian women of today have taken many strides towards business ownership. The broad classification of women business owners include women who establish, inherit, or acquire a business; women who start businesses with spouses or business partners but are either at the forefront or behind the scenes; and finally, women who start fast-growing or part-time or slow-growing firms.

The majority of women business owners operate enterprises in the service sectors, whereas the majority of male business owners operate enterprises in non service sectors, particularly manufacturing. Women are not only achieving economic independence and wealth creation for themselves, but through job creation, they are also providing opportunities for others, particularly for other women.[4] In spite of the growing number of female entrepreneurs, the share of female entrepreneurs is still significantly low when compared to their participation rate. However, there are several factors responsible for increasing the level of female entrepreneurship in India, namely Nature of Entrepreneurship, Motivation, Empowerment, Social Conditions, Economic Conditions, Literacy and Education etc. Below chart reflects the urge for entrepreneurship and motivates the women to become an entrepreneur.

Women Entrepreneurship In India –At a Glance

Periods	Characteristics of women entrepreneurs
Women Entrepreneurs of Fifties	Compulsorily become entrepreneur to bring bread for family or and to survive the heredity business.
Women Entrepreneurs of Sixties	Small step to start small one-woman enterprise for self occupation but not for attaining economic autonomy or economic self sufficiency.
Women Entrepreneurs of Seventies	Established enterprises not out of compulsions or helplessness but swimming upstream and walking uphill

(Contd...)

Women Entrepreneurs of Eighties	Contributing as equal partner in establishing or running enterprises out of thrust.
Women Entrepreneurs of Nineties	Reflected as qualitatively a different breed of women and appeared as a role model in the entrepreneurial world.
21st Century's Women Entrepreneurs	Women's expertise in sophisticated science and technology industries.

Status of Women Entreprises and SSI Unit Managed by Women In India

The total number of women enterprises in the Total SSI Sector was estimated at 10,63,721 (10.11%). The estimated number of enterprises actually managed by women was 9,95,141 (9.46%). In the States of Mizoram, Orissa, Karnataka, Goa, Lakshadweep, Kerala, Tamil Nadu and Pondicherry, the share of women employment was significantly higher (more than 20%). (*See Table 7.1 on next page*)

The total number of female employees in the SSI sector is estimated at 33,17,496. About 57.62 per cent of the female employees were employed in the SSI units located in the States of Tamil Nadu, Kerala, Karntaka, West Bengal and Andhra Pradesh.

The proportion of female employees in the total employment in the SSI sector was of the order of 13.31 per cent. In the States of Mizoram, Orissa, Karnataka, Goa, Lakshadweep, Kerala, Tamil Nadu and Pondicherry, the share of women employment was significantly higher (more than 20%) compared to the total employment in the respective States.

From the Table 7.2, (*See on page 97*) it is seen that about 13 per cent of the women enterprises were in the registered SSI sector and the remaining 87 per cent were in the unregistered SSI sector. With regard to the enterprises managed by women, 11.5 per cent were in the registered SSI sector and 88.5 per cent were in the unregistered SSI sector.

Table 7.1: Participation of Women in Management/Ownership in SSI Sector, State-wise

Sl. No.	Name of State/UT	No. of Enterprises managed by Women	No. of Women Enterprises	No. of Female employees (both registered and unregistered sector)	Percentage of Female employment in the total employment of the State/UTs
1	2	3	4	5	6
1.	Jammu and Kashmir	5640	5742	11466	7.51
2.	Himachal Pradesh	3515	3722	8150	6.26
3.	Punjab	30190	29068	47770	5.26
4.	Chandigarh	2059	2243	1634	5.46
5.	Uttaranchal	8706	8804	16180	8.28
6.	Haryana	10087	9620	30540	5.52
7.	Delhi	13368	14383	42104	6.72
8.	Rajasthan	29785	36371	61068	7.04
9.	Uttar Pradesh	54491	72667	204424	5.11
10.	Bihar	38170	49443	77261	7.14
11.	Sikkim	30	98	221	16.72
12.	Arunachal Pradesh	131	150	446	12.10

(Contd...)

1	2	3	4	5	6
13.	Nagaland	207	179	3211	5.65
14.	Manipur	9168	10745	23338	17.06
15.	Mizoram	3076	3700	6824	27.46
16.	Tripura	631	863	7619	13.38
17.	Meghalaya	3658	3580	8803	13.42
18.	Assam	11189	11757	26065	6.08
19.	West Bengal	71847	69625	331518	15.28
20.	Jharkhand	7271	7865	14012	5.08
21.	Orissa	33274	38233	224846	24.36
22.	Chhattisgarh	11766	10034	62653	11.78
23.	Madhya Pradesh	62351	68823	141315	10.51
24.	Gujarat	55361	53703	121179	9.57
25.	Daman and Diu and Dadra and Nagar Haveli	167	213	6232	14.83
26.	Maharashtra	80662	100670	241431	11.77

(Contd...)

1	2	3	4	5	6
27.	Andhra Pradesh	77347	77166	330719	15.46
28.	Karnataka	101264	103169	341076	20.81
29.	Goa	677	810	7142	24.37
30.	Lakshadweep	61	67	431	26.31
31.	Kerala	137561	139225	414131	37.15
32.	Tamilnadu	130289	129808	493986	24.48
33.	Pondicherry	1089	1065	8283	23.52
34.	Andaman and Nicobar Islands	53	110	418	5.59
	All India	**995141**	**1063721**	**3317496**	**13.31**

Source: http://www.dcmsme.gov.in/ssiindia/census/ch11.htm23.52

Table 7.2: Classification of SSI Units in India on the Basis of Registration

Sl. No.	Characteristic	Registered Units (in Lakhs)	Unregistered Units (in Lakhs)	Total
1.	Men	12.37 (13.08)	82.20 (86.92)	94.57 (100)
2.	Women	1.38 (12.93)	9.26 (87.07)	10.64
3.	**Total**	**13.75 (13.07)**	**9.26 (86.93)**	**105.21 (100)**

Source: www.smallindustryindia.com/ssiindia/census.htm

(Figures in brackets represent percentages to total)

Women Entrepreneur and Self Help Groups

Women comprise half of human resources they have been identified as key agents of sustainable development and women's equality is as central to a more holistic approach towards stabilizing new patterns and process of development that are sustainable. The contribution of women and their role in the family as well as in the economic development and social transformation are pivotal. Women constitute 90 per cent of total marginal workers of the country. Rural women who are engaged in agriculture form 78 per cent of all women in regular work[5].

Experience of NIRD action research projects reveal that, the operational aspects, such as the extent of enabling that goes into the community self help processes and sharpening the mind set of women. Men and the project administrators are low or critical components that determine their extent to which empowerment may or may not take place. The role of micro-credit is to, improve the socio and economic development of women and improve the status of women in households and communities. The micro entrepreneurships are strengthening the women empowerment and remove the gender inequalities. Self Help Group's micro credit mechanism makes the members to involve in other community development activities. Micro credit is promoting the small scale business enterprises and its major aim is to alleviate poverty by income generating activities among women and poor. Therefore, they could achieve self-sufficiency.

In the study report of National Institute of Rural Development (NIRD) on SHGs in 2004, reported that about 25 per cent of members of SHGs have taken enterprises such as pretty business and non-farm activities and are generated income of more than Rupees 1000-1500 per month.

Now-a-days economic development is one of the factors that have changed the entire scenario of social and cultural environment within the country especially for the women. The rural women are engaged in small-scale entrepreneurship programme with the help of Self Help Groups.

Problems of Rural Women Entrepreneurs

An entrepreneur may face variety of problems in the environment, which can be classified into social problems, entrepreneurial problems, financial problems and problems related to environmental support. An entrepreneur may be attacked by any single problem or there may be an interactive and cumulative effect of number of problems.

Vast majorities of women entrepreneur were fighting with the problem of lack of experience, and majority of non entrepreneurial women were not starting their income generation activity due to inconvenience in procuring raw material. Running the entrepreneur non-profitably and not being able to achieve the breakeven point leads to closure of number of entrepreneurs as found out by Paul (1996[6]) and Bhandari (1996[7]). The similar entrepreneurial problems are identified by other researchers and also reported in one recent study conducted by Kumari, Kaushik and Lodha (2010)8, which indicates that much has not changed in last decades.

Lack of Awareness about Governmental Programmes is another problem of women entrepreneur. A sizeable percentage of entrepreneurial and non-entrepreneurial women do not get information timely. Stimpson (1996[9]) and Sharma (1997[10]) also concluded their findings similarly. This indicates that there still exists a communication gap between the implementers and users after lapse of so many years.

Various financial problems, which are faced by entrepreneurial women includes: Problem in arranging finance at various stages of entrepreneurship, lack of knowledge about government and bank financing schemes, problem of margin money etc. The major problem reported by cent per cent subjects of both the categories was lack of awareness about the procedure of receiving finance.

Mohamed (2001[11]) reported that rapid growth of rural and small scale sector were being marked by some problems *i.e.* technological stagnation, under utilization of capacity, lack of vertical mobility, sickness and high mortality rates, followed by shortage of finance, inadequate facilities of storage, inadequate marketing, stiff competition, low mobility, family responsibilities and, social attributes.

Kollan and Parikh (2005[12]) reported that the problems and constraints experienced by women entrepreneur have resulted in restricting and inhibited the expansion of women enterprises. The major barrier encountered by them includes lack of confidence, working capita and knowledge, and socio-cultural barriers.

Women's family obligations also bar them from becoming successful entrepreneurs in both developed and developing nations. The financial institutions discourage women entrepreneurs on the belief that they can at any time leave their business and become housewives again. The result is that they are forced to rely on their own savings, and loan from relatives and family friends.

Another argument is that women entrepreneurs have low-level management skills. They have to depend on office staffs and intermediaries, to get things done, especially, the marketing and sales side of business. Here there is more probability for business fallacies like the intermediaries take major part of the surplus or profit.

Singh, Prof. Surinder Pal (2008[13]), articulated a few challenges that are faced by women entrepreneurs in India which includes lack of visibility as strategic leaders, differential information and assistance needs , family influences on women entrepreneurs et. The study also reported attitudinal discrimination, apathy from bank officials and lack of managerial knowledge etc stand in the way of women entrepreneurs.

Knowledge of alternative source of raw materials availability and high negotiation skills are the basic requirement to run a business. Getting the raw materials from different souse with discount prices is the factor that determines the profit margin. Lack of knowledge of availability of the raw materials and low-level negotiation and bargaining skills are the factors, which affect women entrepreneur's business adventures.

Women Entrepreneurship in the North East India

The North-Eastern Region of India comprises eight states; Arunachal Pradesh, Assam, Manipur, Meghalaya, Mizoram, Nagaland, Tripura, and Sikkim. Among these, Arunachal Pradesh, Meghalaya, Mizoram, Nagaland and Sikkim are largely hilly and sparsely populated. Other states are only partly hilly in various proportions to the plain land, and relatively thickly populated. Among these latter states, Assam and Tripura have more plain land in proportion to the hilly area. Accordingly, the economic activities in the secondary and the tertiary sectors have grown in proportion to the primary sector in the different states. Manipur, with a long tradition in weaving, sericulture, handicrafts, etc has engaged much larger proportion of workers in the secondary sector, followed by Assam that vies closely with the national figure. On the other end, Arunachal Pradesh, Mizoram and Sikkim have slender engagement of workers in the secondary sector. Nagaland has a poor performance in the tertiary sector. Meghalaya performs slightly better than Nagaland but stands far behind the national figure. Arunachal Pradesh, Manipur and Mizoram are more or less at par with India. It may, however, be noted that the tertiary sector in the NER is largely based on the activities generate through external assistance and not by the primary and secondary activities in the states within. This diverse nature of the NER States has shown the different style of entrepreneurship and growth scenario of the small scale and village industries in the region including the women enterprises. (*See Table 7.3 on next page*).

The gender-wise distribution of entrepreneurs in the NER, first of all, indicates that the percentage of male entrepreneurs is far more than the female entrepreneurs in all states and both sectors, rural and urban (*See Table 7.4 and Table 7.5 on page 103*). In Meghalaya, which is inhabited mostly by the tribes that are matrilineal and perhaps matrifocal too, the male entrepreneurship far exceeds the female

Table 7.3: Participation of Women in Management/Ownership in SSI Sector, North Eastern Region, India

Sl. No.	Name of State/UT	No. of Enterises managed by women	No. of women enterprises	No. of Female employees (both (registered and unregistered sector)	Percentage of female employment in the total employment of the State/UTs
1.	Sikkim	30	98	221	16.72
2.	Arunachal Pradesh	131	150	446	12.10
3.	Nagaland	207	179	3211	5.65
4.	Manipur	9168	10745	23338	17.06
5.	Mizoram	3076	3700	6824	27.46
6.	Tripura	631	863	7619	13.38
7.	Meghalaya	3658	3580	8803	13.42
8.	Assam	11189	11757	26065	6.08
	All India	**995141**	**1063721**	**3317496**	**13.31**

Source: http://www.dcmsme.gov.in/ssiindia/census/ch11.htm23.52

Table 7.4: State-Wise Distribution of SSI Units in North-eastern—India

Sl. No.	Name of State/ UT	Total No of SSI	SSI Owned by Women Entrepreneurs
1.	Sikkim	368	98
2.	Arunachal Pradesh	1252	150
3.	Nagaland	13861	179
4.	Manipur	47999	10745
5.	Mizoram	11116	3700
6.	Tripura	24352	863
7.	Meghalaya	3658	3580
8.	Assam	194379	11757
	All India	**10521190**	**1063721**

Source: http: www.smallindustryindia.com./ssiindia/census

Table 7.5: Gender and Area-wise Entrepreneurship Profile

States	Percentage No. of Units in Rural Areas Managed by			
	Male		Female	
	Rural	Urban	Rural	Urban
Arunachal Pradesh	49.41	30.59	7.06	12.94
Assam	40.46	46.07	7.35	5.63
Manipur	41.77	42.27	11.24	4.72
Meghalaya	44.01	22.96	23.74	9.29
Mizoram	7.69	65.63	2.12	24.56
Nagaland	18.52	68.08	2.12	11.29
Sikkim	34.48	48.28	5.75	11.49
Tripura	52.45	41.92	2.92	2.71
All India	**39.83**	**51.85**	**4.50**	**3.82**

Source: S.K. Mishra, Recent Trend of Village and Small Enterprise Sector Exploring and exploiting its Opportunities in the North Eastern Region of India touching upon its Profile and Barriers

entrepreneurship, although the latter is more prominent there than elsewhere in the NER. In the urban areas of Sikkim, Arunachal Pradesh, Nagaland and Mizoram, female entrepreneurs are more in proportion than those in the rural areas, which indicate that in these states urbanization and economic development have worked in favour of gender equality in economic spheres. In Arunachal Pradesh, Manipur, Tripura and Meghalaya rural entrepreneurship is more vivid, indicating the spread of industrial development beyond urban areas. Particularly in Mizoram and Nagaland, urban entrepreneurship dominates the scene and it appears that the rural areas have remained unattractive. Moreover, it evident from the fact that most of the women enterprises in the NER States are unregistered which is due similar with the all India pattern. (Table 7.6).

Table 7.6: Participation of Women in SSI Sector

States	Unregistered		Registered	
	Enterprises managed by women	Women enterprises	Enterprises managed by women	Women enterprises
Sikkim	0	53	30	45
Arunachal Pradesh	80	87	51	63
Nagaland	130	122	77	57
Manipur	8434	9980	734	765
Mizoram	2346	3007	730	693
Tripura	578	784	53	79
Meghalaya	3018	2929	640	651
Assam	9241	9716	1948	2041
NER	23827	26678	4263	4394
All India	**880780**	**926187**	**114361**	**137534**

Source: Conıplied NEC databank.

Schemes for the Development and Promotion of Women Entrepreneurs in India

In order to encourage more and more women enterprises in the MSE sector, several schemes have been formulated by this Ministry and some more are in the process of being finalized, targeted only at the development of women enterprises in India.

Trade Related Entrepreneurship Assistance and Development Scheme for Women (Tread): With a view to encourage women in setting up their own ventures, government implements a Scheme, namely, "Trade Related Entrepreneurship Assistance and Development (TREAD) during the 11th Plan. The scheme envisages economic empowerment of women through the development of their entrepreneurial skills in non-farm activities.

Micro and Small Entreprises Cluster Development Programme (MSE-CDP): The Cluster Development Programme (CDP) being implemented envisages diagnostic study of identified clusters of traditional skill-based MSEs to identify appropriate technologies and their providers and to facilitate adoption of available technology meeting the specific needs of the end users. The Cluster Development aims at enhanced competitiveness, technology improvement, adoption of best manufacturing practices, marketing of products, employment generation etc.

Credit Guarantee Fund Scheme for Micro And Small Entreprises: The Scheme was launched in August 2000 to ensure better flow of credit to micro and small enterprises by minimizing the risk perception of financial institutions and banks in lending without collateral security. Under the scheme, guarantee cover is provided to collateral free credit facility extended by member lending institutions (MLIs) to the new as well as existing micro and small enterprises on loans up to Rs.50 lakh.

Support For Entrepreneurial and Managerial Development: MSME-DIs regularly organize a number of Entrepreneurship

Skill Development Programme (ESDPs)/ Entrepreneurship Development Programme (EDPs)/ Management Development Programmes (MDPs) to train the potential entrepreneurs in improving their techno/managerial knowledge and skill with a view to facilitating them to start MSEs in various fields. Many of the programmes are tailor made for the target group for SC, ST, OBC, Women, Minorities and other weaker sections and exclusively for women also. These programmes are also called 'Out-reach Programmes' as they are conducted in rural/ less developed areas.

Exhibitions for Women Under Promotional Package for Micro and Small Enterprises Approved By CCEA Under Marketing Support: DC (MSME) has formulated a scheme for women entrepreneurs to encourage Small and Micro manufacturing units owned by women and register in DI/DIC in their efforts at tapping and developing overseas markets, to increase participation of representatives of small/micro manufacturing enterprises under MSME stall at International Trade Fairs/ Exhibitions, to enhance export from such units.

Schemes For The Development and Promotion of Women Entrepreneurs in North East India

There are today a large number of organizations like North Eastern Industrial and Technical Consultancy Organization (NEITCO), National Institute of Small Industry Extension Training (NISIET) [till it was merged with the Indian Institute of Entrepreneurship (IIE)] and the North Eastern Industrial Consultants Ltd (NECON) who has been actively involved in entrepreneurship development activities in the region. Their efforts have been supported by the North Eastern Council (NEC) in general and financial institutions like Industrial Development Bank of India (IDBI), Small Industries Development Bank of India (SIDBI), North Eastern Development Finance Corporation Limited (NEDFi) and various commercial banks in particular.

The Ministry of MSME is actively promoting the development of MSMEs in the NER through the programmes and schemes being implemented by its attached office, public sector enterprise, statutory bodies and autonomous organisations, namely, Micro, Small and Medium Enterprise-Development Organisation (MSME-DO), the National Small Industries Corporation Ltd. (NSIC), the Khadi and Village Industries Commission (KVIC), the Coir Board and three national level entrepreneurship development institutes particularly, Indian Institute of Entrepreneurship (IIE), Guwahati. Table 7.7 depicts current data about the Government sponsored development schemes for women entrepreneurs in the NER.

Table 7.7: State-wise Number of Village Industry Units Set up by Women Entrepreneurs and Margin Money Provided under Rural Employment Generation Programme (REGP) in NER, (2005-06 to 2007-08)

States	Margin money disbursed to women entrepreneurs (Rs. in Lakh)			Number of village units set up by women entrepreneurs		
	2005-06	2006-07	2007-08	2005-06	2006-07	2007-08
Arunachal Pradesh	0.00	43.33	149.88	29	26	82
Assam	288.71	515.20	441.48	546	479	450
Manipur	9.5	38.40	18.12	19	41	22
Meghalaya	76.85	84.18	193.97	103	67	165
Mizoram	185.53	313.08	621.51	119	297	486
Nagaland	83.00	97.67	202.17	91	94	212
Sikkim	38.55	45.44	65.69	55	27	112
Tripura	49.18	37.21	110.48	30	26	38

Source: Lok Sabha Unstarred Question No. 2661, dated 16.12.2008.

Task Ahead

Women Entrepreneur has been recognized during the last decade as an important untapped source of economic growth. Women Entrepreneurs create new jobs for themselves and others and by being different also provide society with different solutions to management, organization and business problems as well as to the exploitation of Women Entrepreneurial opportunities. There exists a market failure discriminating against Women possibility to become Women Entrepreneurs and their possibility to become successful Women Entrepreneurs. This market failure needs to be addressed by policy makers so that the economic potential of this group can be fully utilized. Recent efforts initiated by the OECD (1997, 2000) are responses to this lack of knowledge and have focused the attention of policy makers and was on this important topic. The following key strategies may help to foster women entrepreneurship in India:

(a) ***Promoting women entrepreneurs in micro enterprises:*** An increasingly large number of women in India are engaged in the informal economy and operating in the small scale sector, cottage industries, and micro enterprises. With proper governmental and societal support, these women can create sustainable, organized and growth oriented enterprises with a long vision.

(b) ***Institutional and policy based support:*** Government policies and regulations regarding business and industry can be formulated with the intent to encourage women entrepreneurs. There should be a system of reviewing the existing regulatory framework, and make necessary correction. Secondly, the administrative hurdles that have been facing by the women entrepreneurs must be simplified. Thirdly, introduction of simplified and confessional financing for women entrepreneurial project. Finally, promotional and motivating ways for women entrepreneur needs to be undertaken particularly from women's organisations.

(c) ***Directing women entrepreneurs into high growth areas:*** Another main part of the strategy must be to facilitate the entry of women entrepreneurs into the areas where high growth is expected. Special incentives, tax rebate/ holidays, duty cuts and subsidized plant and machinery can be provided to encourage women in emerging sectors.

(d) ***Education and training programme:*** Higher educational incentives for rural women and advanced training programme for development of managerial and technical skills among rural women is a must. Existing women's organisation and women cells may come forward in the direction of forwarding this type of advanced training programme in association with the existing EDP institute.

(e) Private Sector Participation: Private sector can also contribute in its own way to women's entrepreneurial participation in the economy. They can provide various support services to the women entrepreneurs in respect of disseminating information and can help in the capacity building of the entrepreneurs.

References

1. Nazar Mohideen 2005. *Women Entrepreneurship and Small Scale Industries.* New Delh: Himalaya Publishing House.
2. Tuladhar G 1996. Factors Affecting Women Entrepreneurship in Small and Cottage Industries in India Opportunities and Constraints. Internet : http : //www.globalhemp.com /news : 80/05. 142000/ Small scale 48948.htm.
3. Available at www. Decentralization, 2004 Govt. role / training / strength / SHG.htm.
4. Singh ,Prof. Surinder Pal,"*An Insight into the emergence of Women-owned Business as an Economic Force in India*"; 2008-SC1-0166.
5. Sathiabama. K, April 2010, "*Rural Women Empowerment and Entrepreneurship Development*".
6. Paul E 1996. *Entrepreneurship Development*. New Delh: Himalaya Publishing House.
7. Bhandari K, "Participation of Rural Artisan Couples in Selected Trade and Problems by Them ,1996." *M.Sc. Thesis, Unpublished*. Bikaner: R.A.U.
8. Sujata Kumari, (2010) Vandana Kaushik and Neeta Lodha "Problems Faced by Rural Women Entrepreneurs of Rajasthan" Home Comm Sci, 4(2): 115-119.
9. Stimpson, D.V, 1996, " Attitudial Characteristics of Male and Female Entrepreneurs in USA & India" , *Journal of Psychological Studies*, 38(2): 64:68
10. Sharma, R 1997, " Economic Feasibility of Establishing a Small Scale Fruit and Vegetable Processing Unit" *M.Sc., Thesis, Unpublished,* Hisar CCS Harayanna Agrl. University.

11. Mohamed HS 2001. Problems of Rural Industries. *Kisan World,* 28(2): 49.

12. Kollan , Bharti and Parikh, Indira J, 2005 "A Refection of Indian Women in Entrepreneurial World", IIM, WPNo. 2005-08-07, p. 1.

13. Singh, Prof. Surinder Pal, 2008, "An Insight into the Emergence of Women Owned Business as an Economic Force in India", SCI -0166.

14. Ganguly M 2001. Role of Women in Entrepreneurial Development. *Social Change,* 20: 36-39.

15. Mishra, S. K., Recent Trend of Village and Small Enterprise Sector: Exploring and Exploiting its Opportunities in the North Eastern Region of India Touching Upon its Profile and Barriers (June 29, 2007). Available at SSRN: http://ssrn.com/abstract=997310.

16. Govt. of India (2003) Third All India Census of Small Scale Industries 2001-2002, Development Commissioner, SSI, Ministry of Small Scale Industries, Govt. of India, New Delhi.

17. Govt. of India (2006) Annual Report 2005-06, Ministry of SSI , Govt. of India, New Delhi.

18. Mishra, S.K. (2007) "Analysis of Gender Disparity in Meghalaya by Various Types of Composite Indices", Social Science Research Network, SSRN: http://ssrn.com/abstract=994669.

19. Sachdeva, G. (2006) "India's North-East: Rejuvenating A Conflict-Riven Economy", http://www.manipuronline.com/Economy/February2006/conflictriveneconomy06_1.htm

20. Srinath, T.T. (2002) "The Emerging Personality of a Small-Scale Entrepreneur", *Business Line* (Internet Edition) May 21.

21. Decentralisation 2004.Internet Link http://www the Indian Experience:Government's Role Decentralization Govt. role/training/strength/SHG.htm. (Retrieved on7.10.2006).

22. Lalita .N, (2005) "Micro Finance and Rural Development", Gandhigram Rural Institute, Gandhigram, Dindigal, Tamilnadu.

23. Meenu Agrawal, Shobana Nelasco (2009) "Empowerment of Rural Women in India" Kanishka Publishers, New Delhi.

24. Ram Naresh Thakur (2009). "Rural Women Empowerment in India" in Empowerment of RuralWomen in India Kanishka Publishers, New Delhi.

25. Shobana Nelasco & Junofy Antorozarina (2009) "Rural women empowerment through Self Help Groups" in Empowerment of Rural Women in India Kanishka Publishers, New Delhi.

26. Prabha Singh (2009) "Rural Women and Development of Entrepreneurship with Special Reference to Punjab" in Empowerment of Rural Women in India Kanishka Publishers, New Delhi.

27. Lipi (2009) "Women Empowerment: Globalization and Opportunities" in Empowerment of RuralWomen in India Kanishka Publishers, New Delhi.

Self Help Groups and Rural Women Entrepreneurship
Issues and Challenges

Aparajita Biswal

ABSTRACT

Women entrepreneurship through SHG based micro-finance has been central to development agenda in India. Indian Government has also paid special attention to women's empowerment. Women's empowerment encompasses their enhanced status in social, political and economic spheres. Though, micro credit for poverty reduction has been accepted as a major tool in development discourse, however, women's empowerment through micro credit programmes has been limited. No doubt, the micro-finance based women empowerment programmes have greater impact on women's empowerment, however, their effective functioning and performance assessment is always felt imperative for policy decisions. Micro-credit is increasingly hailed as a panacea for poverty alleviation. While micro-credit has, in some circumstances, contributed positively to women's empowerment and helped extremely poor women survive economic crises in the short term, it is now increasingly recognized that micro-credit interventions have concentrated only on the economic aspects of poverty and not addressed its non-economic dimensions. It has been rightly argued that since some credit programmes foster group formation and enable women to generate income, they offer potential for both political and economic empowerment. However, since credit by itself cannot overcome patriarchal systems of control at household and community levels, this potential is not always realized.

Micro-credit works when other empowerment strategies are included as part of social mobilization. These strategies have included assisting women to have increased control over their incomes and resources, helping women to define their own priorities, and ensuring their participation in decision-making at various levels: household, community, region and state.

The self-help group (SHGs) are empowering the rural poor by providing them access to institutional credit and other relevant services. The SHGs lay stress on thrift, training and capacity building. Emphasis is placed on educating the members on social issues also. Provision of credit through SHGs has produced many positive results. The problem of over dues has been solved. The borrowers need not only credit, but also supporting inputs and services. In short, micro-finance led to the real empowerment of the rural poor, particularly women. Empowerment and entrepreneurship needs to be an integral part of policies which should not be assumed to be an automatic outcome of micro finance programmes, whether designed for financial sustainability or poverty targeting. It has demonstrated the potential of building the social capital of the poorest communities and goes a long way to meet the survival credit and provide for sustainable livelihoods.

Introduction

In the 21st century women contribute a major share to the emerging economy of our country. In India, the numbers of women employees have been increasing. There are quite a good numbers of Indian women who have proved themselves quite successful in many fields. The liberalization of the economy in the early 1990s has opened the way for a large number of persons to become entrepreneurs and the post-liberalization and globalization era has brought with it a growing middle class economy.

Any developed country cannot ignore the role of women in economic development. Women constitute about half of the population. The state does not discriminate them on the basis of sex. They have equal rights in all spheres of life. It is well recognized that attainment of any sustainable development cannot be secured without full participation and integration of women in all spheres of life and development of action plan to uplift socio-economic condition of women. Development of society is directly related to income generation capacity of its members. With agriculture as key income generation activity the entrepreneurship based on it can directly affect the income of a major chunk of our population. Developing small entrepreneurship is the only solution to the problems of unemployment and proper utilization of human and other resources. So entrepreneurship is a recent phenomenon and the emerging reality in new growing economy.

Women Entrepreneurship and Its' Strategies

Women Entrepreneurs are the women or a group of women who initiate, organize and operate a business enterprise. The Government of India notes women entrepreneurs as "an enterprise owned and controlled by women having a minimum financial interest of 51 per cent of the capital and giving at least 51 per cent of the employment generated in the enterprise to women". Women take into entrepreneurship due to various reasons. Lack of sufficient employment opportunities in organized sector forced women to seek alternatives in entrepreneurship. It is the collective forces of education, work experience, exposure and urbanization provides impetus to women to something non-traditional like entering into opening up their own ventures. Women entrepreneurship not only generates-income for her but also generates employment for others. In turn, it improves the standard of living of the society and also solves the problems of unemployment to some extent.

When women moves forward, the family moves, the village moves and the nation moves which gives a strong economical status to the country. In the present global competitive business and industrial situation the women entrepreneurs can play a great role and emerge themselves.

Strategies for Women Entrepreneurship

Women have the strong confidence and potential to establish enterprise of their own. While talking about women entrepreneurship, the theme has been conceived with the following strategies in mind:

- Initiative for entrepreneurial awareness;
- Promoting self-employment;
- Adequate training and supporting facilities;
- Providing lean season wage employment;
- Adequate training and supporting facilities;
- Providing savings habit among women;
- Providing a range of support service to meet gender needs;
- Addressing minimum needs such as nutrition, health, sanitation, housing and education;
- Direct involvement of women in the development programmes.

Rural Women and Entrepreneurship

The problems of rural women are specific. They are unaware of their rights, duties, responsibilities and opportunities. They suffered from many disadvantages in comparison to urban women in terms of literacy rates, labour participation, rates of earning etc. All the efforts of the government, financial institutions and other agencies to promote entrepreneurship concentrate on urban women. Rural women have been neglected all the times. Efforts have been made to develop entrepreneurship among them. Development of women will become reality only when the rural women are developed. The speed of development in an economy cannot be accelerated unless the women do not come forward and play their significant role in the society. So the awaking of Indian women, particularly rural women are inevitable for socio-economic development of the country.

Approaches and Emergence of SHGs

With the new emphasis given to micro and small enterprises, the self employment activities and household enterprises are considered as essential factors for achieving socio-economic development in the developed and developing countries. According to world economic report 2006, global growth has been largely affected by the financial conditions and continued accommodative policies with the emerging economies and developing countries strengthening the growth momentum in the latter half of 2005. Indian economy registers a growth rate of 8.1 per cent in 2004, 8.3 per cent in 2005 and projected growth rate of 7.3 per cent in 2006. Orissa, despite its abundant resources both natural and human, has been one of the poorest states in the country with almost 50 per cent of its people living below the poverty line.

The high level dependence on informal sector and non-institutional sources continued despite rapid growth of the banking network in the last five decades. In this background NABARD conducted studies in the mid eighties. Based on the studies and action research conducted, NABARD developed the Self Help Groups (SHGs) and bank linkage approach as the core strategy that could be used by banking system in India to outreach to poor.

Concept of SHGs

- SHGs are a small group of rural poor, who have voluntarily come forward to form a group for improvement of the social and economic status of the members.
- It can be formal (registered) or informal.
- The concept unde3rlines the principle of Thrift, Credit and Self Help.
- Members of SHG agree to save regularly and contribute to a common fund.
- The members agree to use this common fund and such other funds (like grants and loans from banks), which

they may receive as a group, to give small loans to needy members as per the decision of the group.

- To mobilize the resources of the individual members for their collective economic development.
- To uplift the living conditions of the poor.
- To create a habit of savings.
- Utilization of local resources.
- To mobilize individual skills for group's interest.
- To assist the members financially at the time of need.
- Entrepreneurship development.
- To identify problems, analyzing and finding solutions in the group.
- To act as a media for socio-economic development of the village.
- To develop linkages with institutions of NGOs.
- To develop leadership qualities.
- To use as an effective delivery channel for rural credit

Exhibit-2: Nature and Functions of SHGs Operating In India

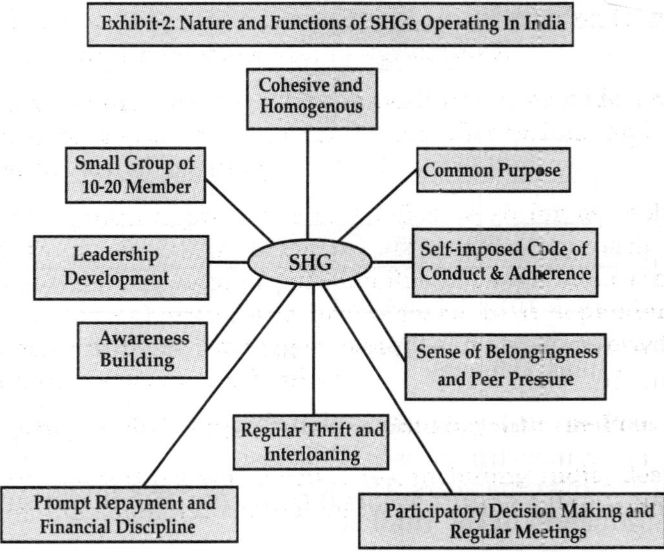

The SHG in India are mainly operated with the objective of social mobilization and economic activation of the demoralized sections of the rural sector. Micro-credit programmes through their inherent and in built developmental approach contribute to the socio-economic empowerment of rural women by enhancing small entrepreneurship activities. The SHG operation in India can be reflected by a relation as follows: The above relationship reflects a high degree of socio-economic mobilization of utilized and underutilized resources of the rural economic of India.

Over the years the SHG – Bank Linkage has been increased tremendously. In this connection the effort of NABARD is simply remarkable which leads financing as well as outreach activities. The following table shows the growth indicators of SHG - bank linkage programme and compound annual growth rate of it.

Growth Indicators of SHG Bank-Linkage Programme in India

No.	Particulars /Year	1997-98	2004-05	CAGR (%)
1.	SHGs Linked (No.)	5,719	797457	102.46
2.	Families I Assisted (No. in million)	0.24	11	73.15
3.	Bank Loan (Rs. In million)	119	29942	120.27
4.	Refinance Assistance (Rs. Million)	107	19678	90.32
5.	Average Loan / SHG (Rs.)	2081	37547	8.80
6.	Average Loan/Family (Rs.	203	2673	8.75
7.	Participating Banks (No.)	150	573	21.10
8.	Partner NGDs (No.)	291	4323	47.03

Source: Micro-Finance, A Strategy for Alleviation of Poverty, J. Lenka and K. C. Mishra OEJ, 2008.

The above table reflects that there has been a potential increase in the number of SHG linked, Family Assisted, Bank Loan, etc. over the years. This shows a positive impact on the transformation of the rural society.

Orissa is also not lag behind the micro-finance activities. There has been a cumulative growth of SHG—Bank Linkage in the state over the years which is reflected in the following table.

Cumulative Growth of SHGs Linked to Banks in Orissa *Vis-a-Vis* India

Region	2001	2002	2003	2004	2005	2006
Orissa	8888	20553	42272	77588	123256	180896
All India	263825	461478	717360	1079091	1618456	2238565
Per cent	3.4	4.5	5.9	7.2	7.6	8.1

Source: Reducing Poverty through Micro Finance: A Perspective on Self Help Groups in Orissa, Dr. K. H. Badatya & Mrs. K. C. Badatya , OEJ, 2008.

Commercial Banks and RRBs have been the measure players of this SHG Bank-Linkage programme. These banks have been engaged in extending loans to the SHG for undertaking various entrepreneur activities. They reach the people with much co-operation and assist them so that they will feel safe and secured to initiate any project or activity for their socio-economic empowerment.

Agencies	Orissa			India				
	No. of SHGs	Per cent	Bank Loan	Per cent	No. of SHGs	Per cent	Bank Loan	Per cent
CBs	77859	43.0	2140.1	45.0	1188040	53.1	69874.5	61.3
RRBs	86256	47.7	2216.9	46.6	740024	33.1	33221.5	29.1
Coops	16781	9.3	397.7	8.4	310501	13.9	10879.5	9.5
Total	**180896**	**100.0**	**4754.7**	**100.0**	**22338565**	**100.0**	**113976**	**100.0**

Source: Reducing Poverty through Micro Finance: A Perspective on Self Help Groups in Orissa, Dr. K. H. Badatya & Mrs. K. C. Badatya , OEJ, 2008.

The above table shows that RRBs have captured the rural credit sector more proportionately in comparison to Commercial Banks and Co-operative Banks in Orissa. But the All India figure shows that Commercial Banks are the leading banks to continue the same operation.

Sustainable and Sustainability of Entrepreneurship

The business community has the contributions towards a sustainable world. In addition to integrating across fields, sustainability must also be integrated across sectors or interests. It is clear that governments alone have neither the will not the capability to accomplish sustainability on their own. The private sector, as the engine of economic activity on the planet, and major source for creativity, innovation and entrepreneurship, further, entrepreneurship towards the sustainability context, the role of social entrepreneurship for the preservation and positive development of the basic infrastructure is most vital.

All the aspects have been created and added to the multi-faceted concept of entrepreneurship with these extensions and new connections with ecological and social as new tags, still leaves us unsatisfied when brought to the sustainability context. There is a risk of treating these kinds of specific categories of entrepreneurial behaviors to miss the holistic, integrated approach implied by the sustainability paradigm. Taking together sustainability with entrepreneurship invites us to a new stand of conversation. In this dialogue we try to grasp the phenomenon where we use business organizing as a means to create solutions and opportunities of the agenda imposed by the movements created by the sustainable development discourse. The key work to guide as further is integration — to integrate social, ecological and economical aspects with entrepreneurial behaviour.

Sustainable entrepreneurship attaching an attribute to the "generic" entrepreneurial process. Sustainability requires "and", as in "ecological and social objectives" — the integrated meaning that follows from and is implied by the sustainability approach. If only one of he two optional dimensions besides the economical "entrepreneurships — usual" is present, then it would reflect the case more clear to stick to either co-partnership or social entrepreneurship, respectively. Sustainability entrepreneurship — by forming the concept sustain entrepreneurship; the use of entrepreneurial activity in a determined action orientation towards solving sustainability — related problem with business organizing as a means to solve the problem(s) – "business with a cause": To turn business activity from a part of the problem to a part of the solution.

Challenges Ahead

The entrepreneurs are expecting more from financial institutions particularly obtaining timely micro-credit as well as institutions to co-ordinate activities of rural women entrepreneurs. They need more education, training and consultancy both from government and non-governmental organizations which can improve their social status and make them more self confident by removing inferiority complex in them. They are also expecting promotional help like preparation of the project report, registration, licensing, etc for starting small enterprises to get better value for their products. They are expecting more support from their family as well as from the society. They are willing to leave their villages and attend training courses at the far off places to start their own business. Since most of the rural women are weak and do not have adequate resources to start, the SHGs should come forward to help them.

Emergence of entrepreneurship is a process dependent of several interrelated factors. These factors do not help much to the rural women to emerge as entrepreneurs. An individual rural woman is uneducated, unskilled, and her upbringing denies herself confidence, need for achievement and independence. The govt. policies and programmes are not sufficiently oriented towards her and support activities are not well directed towards rural women entrepreneurs. So an integrated approach is needed to develop and promote entrepreneurship among rural women. Rural women are having basic indigenous knowledge, skill, potential and resources to establish and manage home enterprises and traditional cottage industries. What more they need is awareness, motivation, technical skill and support from family, government and other organizations to promote entrepreneurial skill among them. With the right assistance at right time, they can strengthen their capacities besides adding to the family income and national productivity.

Conclusion

The role SHGs as a group is very crucial in helping out the micro enterprises on a sustainable basis. They have to get themselves updated with required information. Acquisition and dissemination of market related information to group members is one of the important functions of the SHGs. The promoters of the groups need to sensitize them at regular basis. Groups need to maintain proper record of financial transactions and members should also to follow this for their enterprises. Very often it is found that members mix up their personal transaction with the business which creates confusion about the health of the enterprise. Group leaders need to guide the members in this direction also. Proper training to group leaders and if possible to other members will go long way in helping out solving many above mentioned problems of the micro enterprise.

Bankers and other MFIs need to scale up their non-financial support along with the micro credit infusion. Particularly bankers in NER have a greater role as other MFIs are not operating in many numbers. NER has tremendous potential for micro enterprise creation. The diversity of culture which provides enough space for innovative products and the availability of abundant natural resources which provides necessary inputs for those products need to be matched and the role of SHGs in bridging these two ends through a entrepreneurial revolution in this part of India is very much possible.

References

1. Adams Dale, W. and A. Delbert (1992), *Fitchett Informal Finance in Law Income Countries*, Oxford: West View Press.

2. Aloysuis Prakash Fernandez, (1994), The Myrada Experience: Alternate Management Systems for Savings and Credit of the Rural Poor, Bangalore: The Mysore Resettlement and Development Agency.

3. Batliwala, Srilatha, (1994), "The Meaning of Empowerment New Concept from Action", In Adrienna Germain, Gita Sen and Lincoln Chen (eds.), Population Policies Reconsidered: Health, Empowerment and Rights, Cambridge, Macs: Harward School of Public Health.

4. Calman, Leslie, J. (1992), *Towards Empowerment: Women and Movement Policies in India*, New York: Westview Press.

5. Chen, Martha, A. (1996), (ed.) *Beyond Credit: A Subsector Approach to Promoting Women's Enterpries*, Canada, Ottawa: Aga Khan Foundation.

6. Ela Bhatt, (1997), "*Women and Development Alternatives, Micro and Small Scale Enterprises in India*" in (ed.). Louise, Dignard and Jose Hennet, *Women in Micro and Small Scale Enterprise Development*, San Fransico: Westview Press.

7. Gupta, R.C. (1994), *Management of Savings and Credit Programmes by NGOs*, New Delhi: Har-Anand Publications.

8. Gupta, S.P., (1996), *Statistical Methods*, New Delhi: Sultan Chand and Sons, pp. 3-9.

9. Hans, Dieter Siebel, (2000),"*Agricultural Development Banks Close Them on Reform them*", *Finance and Development*, Washington D.C. International Monetary Fund, pp. 45-47.

10. Howarth Rhona and Langdon Keren, (2000), *Organising Self Help Groups*, New Delhi: Department of Women and Child Development, Government of India.

11. Karmakar, K.G. (1999), *Rural Credit and Self Help Groups: Micro-Finance Needs and Concepts in India*. New Delhi: Sage Publications.

Women Entrepreneur
Bright Outlook for Women

Dr. Veershetty G. Rathod

ABSTRACT

Women constitute almost half of the total population of world. Similarly in India also women constitute 50 per cent of the total population. Till the turn of the century, man has enjoyed a dominant position. But change in position technological innovation and modern way of thinking can reduce the disparity between men and women, and bring about equality and equity between them, the need of the hour in women empowerment both through provision of employment and enterprise creation. Typologically, the former leader to endogenous empowerment and the latter give rise to exogenous empowerment. Women entreprenurer's have been making a significant impact in all segments of the economy in Canada, Great Britain, Germany Australia and US. The areas choosen by women are retail trade, restaurants, hotels, education, cultural, cleaning insurance and manufacturing. It is the group of women or single women running an enterprise or company in order to earn profit. Now-a-days because of women empowerment women are stepping-stone into the industries and are taking the place of men. Now-a-day's women are running several business-like beauty parlours, tailoring shops, boutiques, etc. Women entrepreneurs may be defined as a woman or a group of women who initiate, organize and run a business enterprise. In terms of Schunpeterian concept of innovative entrepreneurs, women who innovate, initiate or adopt a business activity are called business entrepreneur.

Introduction

Women constitute almost half of the total population of world. Similarly in India also women constitute 50 per cent of the total population. Till the turn of the century, man has enjoyed a dominant position. But change in position technological innovation and modern way of thinking can reduce the disparity between man and women, and bring about equality and equity between them, the need of the hour in women empowerment both through provision of employment and enterprise creation. Typologically, the former leader to endogenous empowerment and the latter give rise to exogenous empowerment. Women entreprenurer's have been making a significant impact in all segments of the economy in Canada, Great Britain, Germany, Australia and US. The areas choosen by women are retail trade, restaurants, hotels, education, cultural, cleaning insurance and manufacturing. It is the group of women or single women running an enterprise or company in order to earn profit. Now-a-days because of women empowerment women are stepping-stone into the industries and are taking the place of men. Now-a-day's women's are running several business like beauty parlours, tailoring shops, boutiques, etc. Women entrepreneurs may be defined as a woman or a group of women who initiate, organize and run a business enterprise. In terms of Schunpeterian concept of innovative entrepreneurs, women who innovate, initiate or adopt a business activity are called business entrepreneur.

The Government of India has defined women entrepreneurs based on women participation in equity and employment of a business enterprise. Accordingly, a woman entrepreneur is defined as an enterprise owned and controlled by a woman having a minimum financial interest of 51 per cent of the capital and giving at least 51 per cent of the employment generated in the enterprise to a woman. India-based women entrepreneurs might be in for great times ahead. State minister for Major Industries, Commerce and Export Promotion and Food Processing in Andhra Pradesh (AP),

Kanna Lakshminarayana, has stressed upon the need for promoting women entrepreneurship in the state. Meanwhile, similar initiatives have been undertaken by the Hassan Special Economic Zone in Karnataka, which has decided to promote women empowerment in the state as part of its corporate social responsibility (CSR) initiative.

Speaking to a Bizxchange correspondent, P Girija, secretary of the Confederation of Women Entrepreneurs (COWE), said, "Only about five per cent of women in AP are currently working as entrepreneurs. There is a need to encourage more women to take up entrepreneurship and for that the AP government has come up with a policy that will encourage women to set up their own small businesses. Also, more projects and opportunities need to be generated for women SME owners in the state."

Notably, AP women entrepreneurs are entitled to 5 per cent additional investment subsidy up to Rs. 5 lakh and 10 per cent land reservation in Andhra Pradesh Industrial Infrastructure Corporation (APIIC)-developed industrial estates/parks, among such other benefits.

In this context, Anindita Hazarika, owner of owner of H2 A2 Creations, a small-sized unit in Guwahati, which manufactures and supplies home furnishings and handicraft products, said, "Why just AP, women entrepreneurship should be encouraged in all states across India. Although the government offers various benefits to SME owners like us, there is an inherent bias in the society, which seeks to prevent business growth of enterprises run by women. A surge in the number of women-run organisations throughout the country could help remove that bias."

They have made their Marks in Business Because of the following Reasons

- They want to improve their mettle in innovation and competitive jobs;
- They want the change to control the balance between their families and responsibility and their business levels;

- They want new challenges and opportunities for self-fulfillment.

Role of Women as an Entrepreneur's

Imaginative: It refers to the imaginative approach or original ideas with competitive market. Well-planned approach is needed to examine the existing situation and to identify the entrepreneurial opportunities. It further implies that women entrepreneurs have association with knowledgeable people and contracting the right organisation offering support and services.

Attribute to Work hard: Enterprising women have further ability to work hard. The imaginative ideas have to come to a fair play. Hard work is needed to build up an enterprise..

Persistence: Women entrepreneurs must have an intention to fulfill their dreams. They have to make a dream transferred into an idea enterprise; Studies show that successful women work hard.

Ability and Desire to Take Risk: The desire refers to the willingness to take risk and ability to the proficiency in planning making forecast estimates and calculations.

Profit Earning Capacity: She should have a capacity to get maximum return out of invested capital.

A Woman Entrepreneur has also to Perform All the Functions Involved in Establishing an Enterprise

These include idea generation, and screening, determination of objectives, project preparation, product analysis, determination of forms of business organisation, completion of formal activities, raising funds, procuring men machine materials and operations of business.

Push-Pull Factors and Women in Business

Women in business are a recent phenomenon in India. By and large they had confide themselves to petty business and tiny cottage industries. Women entrepreneurs engaged in business due to push and pull factors. Which encourage women to have an independent occupation and stands on their own legs. A sense towards independent decision-making on their life and career is the motivational factor behind this urge. Saddled with household chores and domestic responsibilities women want to get independence Under the influence of these factors the women entrepreneurs choose a profession as a challenge and as an urge to do something new. Such situation is described as pull factors. While in push factors women engaged in business activities due to family compulsion and the responsibility is thrust upon them.

Five Functions of a Woman Entrepreneur

1. Exploration of the prospects of starting a new business enterprise;
2. Undertaking a risk and handling of economic uncertainties involved in business;
3. Introduction of innovations, imitations of innovations;
4. Co-ordination, administration and control;
5. Supervision and leadership.

In nutshell, women entrepreneur are those women who think of a business enterprise, initiate it organize and combine the factors of production, operate the enterprise, undertake risk and handle economic uncertainties involved in running a business enterprise.

How to Develop Women Entrepreneurs?

Right efforts from all areas are required in the development of women entrepreneurs and their greater participation in the entrepreneurial activities. Following efforts can be taken into account for effective development of women entrepreneurs.

1. Consider women as specific target group for all developmental programmes.

2. Better educational facilities and schemes should be extended to women folk from government part.
3. Adequate training programme on management skills to be provided to women community.
4. Encourage women's participation in decision-making.
5. Vocational training to be extended to women community that enables them to understand the production process and production management.
6. Skill development to be done in women's polytechnics and industrial training institutes. Skills are put to work in training-cum-production workshops.
7. Training on professional competence and leadership skill to be extended to women entrepreneurs.
8. Training and counselling on a large scale of existing women entrepreneurs to remove psychological causes like lack of self-confidence and fear of success.
9. Counselling through the aid of committed NGOs, psychologists, managerial experts and technical personnel should be provided to existing and emerging women entrepreneurs.
10. Continuous monitoring and improvement of training programmes.
11. Activities in which women are trained should focus on their marketability and profitability.
12. Making provision of marketing and sales assistance from government part.
13. To encourage more passive women entrepreneurs the Women training programme should be organized that taught to recognize her own psychological needs and express them.
14. State finance corporations and financing institutions should permit by statute to extend purely trade related finance to women entrepreneurs.

15. Women's development corporations have to gain access to open-ended financing.
16. The financial institutions should provide more working capital assistance both for small scale venture and large scale ventures.
17. Making provision of micro-credit system and enterprise credit system to the women entrepreneurs at local level.
18. Repeated gender sensitization programmes should be held to train financiers to treat women with dignity and respect as persons in their own right.
19. Infrastructure, in the form of industrial plots and sheds, to set up industries is to be provided by state run agencies.
20. Industrial estates could also provide marketing outlets for the display and sale of products made by women.
21. A Women Entrepreneur's Guidance Cell set up to handle the various problems of women entrepreneurs all over the state.
22. District Industries Centres and Single Window Agencies should make use of assisting women in their trade and business guidance.
23. Programmes for encouraging entrepreneurship among women are to be extended at local level.
24. Training in entrepreneurial attitudes should start at the high school level through well-designed courses, which build confidence through behavioral games.
25. More governmental schemes to motivate women entrepreneurs to engage in small scale and large-scale business ventures.
26. Involvement of Non Governmental Organisations in women entrepreneurial training programmes and counselling.

Women Entrepreneur Data

Before analyzing the special traits in successful woman entrepreneurs, a glance at the physiological variations in the brains of men and women can be beneficial:

- Male brains are 10 per cent larger than female brains.
- Female has more nerve cells in certain areas.
- Women transfer data faster due to larger corpus collusum, making it easier for increased flexibility and multitasking.
- Men are left-brain oriented and are largely successful in solving numbers and problems.
- 'Gray matter'—the part that allows thinking is 55.4 per cent in women and 50.8 per cent in men.

This reveals that women are endowed with natural advantages that aid in creating, developing and fostering relationships. Not restricting herself to merely fostering relationships with her family, friends and society, a successful woman uses this proficiency to build and maintain a flourishing business enterprise. She translates her natural advantages into effective networking, excellent communication skills and empathetic behavior. Her mastery over multitasking influences her to initiate action with direction and integrate it with management and organizational skills. A successful woman entrepreneur has the attitude and the inner drive to change her dream, her vision into reality.

The Seven Traits to Success

Successful Entrepreneurs Gain the Respect of their Peers: One of the first and most obvious characteristics you'll see operating in an exceptional entrepreneur is an equitable and unbiased disposition. Plain and simple the successful entrepreneur recognizes that no one is above or below. With an attitude of respect for others, the successful entrepreneur gains the respect from everyone they encounter. Strategies, attitudes and methods filter down to each person and reflect on all actions and activities. A successful entrepreneur gives everyone the space to be great. No matter how effective or beneficial your expertise, becoming a successful entrepreneur requires building up of your character muscles, traits and habits, which correspondingly make your dreams a reality.

Successful Entrepreneurs Believe and Trust in Themselves: The savvy entrepreneur is good at trusting her own ideas and instincts. Starting out as an entrepreneur requires persistence, determination and a high level of self-discipline. Continuing as a successful entrepreneur requires even more persistence, determination and self-discipline. The wise and successful entrepreneur knows this and works hard at developing their level of confidence. If you have a strong code of ethics and believe in yourself, then your ideas can work. Having the desire and passion are the first steps on your journey; getting there requires believing in yourself.

Successful Entrepreneurs Follow a Plan: The successful entrepreneur follows a plan. Haphazard or trial and error have no place for the triumphant entrepreneur, for no one gets to her destination without a map or a guide to follow. That doesn't mean you won't go off course if another road seems better, but it's still more effective to have a plan in place. Most successful entrepreneurs start out by writing a basic business plan that acts as the impetus and guide for their endeavors. It doesn't have to be fancy or lengthy but it should include marketing strategies, goals, intentions, ideas and why you can do better than your competition. A business plan should be reviewed and updated periodically for each new idea stirs and inspires other ideas.

Successful Entrepreneurs Think Creatively: Successful entrepreneurs are not afraid of thinking creatively. Whether a business idea has already been tried makes no difference to the exceptional entrepreneur. She sees better ways of doing things and knows that every idea can be expanded upon, made better, enhanced or broadened. The successful entrepreneur is willing to think outside or the proverbial box, which means using imagination, trying new things and expanding on a vision. The savvy entrepreneur pays careful attention as to whether a particular strategy is working. If after giving it her best shot the entrepreneur realizes the particular strategy isn't working, they know there's no point in continuing to invest energy, time and effort in the strategy. They move on to another approach and idea.

Successful Entrepreneurs Explore Their Exceptional Skills: Successful entrepreneurs realize that we each have our strengths and weaknesses as well as a multitude of skills and talents. Successful people ask themselves often what skills they have that no one shares in quite the same way. An exceptional and successful entrepreneur explores their particular skills until they find the ones that match most closely with their ideal. They don't try to be and do everything. If the successful entrepreneur needs help, they're willing to find someone who can do it better, and allows in the support. The successful entrepreneur stays open to change for they recognize that as they move forward, doors open in unexpected places that carry them to their next level of success.

Successful Entrepreneurs Envision Their Success: The successful entrepreneur gives time to envisioning how they want their business to look and how they want it to be. Intention is a powerful and dynamic tool. For those who are not inclined towards intention and visualization, talk to a successful athlete and you'll discover that before each sporting event, the successful athlete envisions exactly how he or she wants things to turn out. Imagine what it will feel like when you've reached a particular set of goals. Get in touch with the feelings, you'd have as a successful entrepreneur. Practice and conceive of the sense of empowerment and the joy of having succeeded. The successful entrepreneur knows they have the power to live life the way they want, but to make it a reality, they know it has to be seen first.

Successful Entrepreneurs Never Give Up: Giving up is never in the vocabulary of the successful woman entrepreneur. Of course there may be days when a successful entrepreneur feels discouraged or disappointed, but giving up is not an option. Having faith, trust, confidence and determination are the qualities needed for the successful entrepreneur. To keep their focus on track, they seek out the support of those that know them, encourage them and bring out their natural enthusiasm. The smart and successful entrepreneur realizes that there will be good days and not so good days.

Being a successful woman entrepreneur requires accepting the ebbs and flows of business for it is in fact what separates the exceptional and successful entrepreneur from the one who gives up far too soon.

Most Successful Women Entrepreneurs Possess the Following Traits

She is Ambitious: A successful woman entrepreneur is extremely ambitious, has an inner urge or drive to transform an idea into reality. Experience from her previous tenure as an employee, relying on educational qualifications or lessons learnt from inherited business, she is ready to seize opportunities, sets goal, possess clear vision, steps confidently forward and is ambitious to succeed. Every successful woman entrepreneur is truly determined to achieve goals and make her business flourish. In-depth knowledge of the field is essential to success. She comes with new innovative solutions to old problems to tide over issues.

She is Confident: A successful woman entrepreneur is confident in her ability. She is ready to learn from others, seek help from experts if it means adding value to her goals. She is optimistic and is more willing to take risks. A successful woman entrepreneur uses common sense to make sound judgements when encountering everyday situations. This is gleaned from past experience and knowledge acquired over the years. It is essential not to get frustrated and give up when you face obstacles and trials ? a part of setting up any business venture. The ability to explore uncharted territories and take bold decisions is the hallmark of a successful woman entrepreneur. A successful woman usually loves what she does. She is extremely passionate about her tasks and activities. Her high energy levels motivate her to contribute immensely towards building, establishing and maintaining a thriving business.

She is Open and Willing to Learn: A successful woman entrepreneur keeps abreast of changes, as she is fully aware of the importance of evolving changes. She is ahead of her competitors and thrives on changes. She adapts her business to changes in technology or service expectations of her clients. She is curious, interested to learn and accommodative to innovations.

She is Cost Conscious: A successful woman entrepreneur prepares realistic budget estimates. She provides cost-effective quality services to her clients. With minimized cost of operations, she is able to drive her team to maximize profits and reap its benefits.

She Values Teamwork and Loyalty: She has the ability to work with all levels of people. She is keen on maintaining relationships and communicates clearly and effectively. This helps her to negotiate even sensitive issues easily. She is empathetic to people around her and possess good networking skills that help her to expand contacts and make use of opportunities.

She can Balance Home and Work: Cautious of not becoming a workaholic, a successful woman entrepreneur is good at balancing diverse aspects of life. Her multi-tasking ability combined with support from spouse and family members enables her to blend business priorities with family and household responsibilities efficiently and effectively.

She is Conscious of her Responsibility to Society: A successful woman entrepreneur is willing to share her success with the society. She is committed to help others and enjoys doing it.

It is no wonder that millions of aspiring woman entrepreneurs admire Oprah Winfrey for her entrepreneurial skills, business achievements, and commitment to philanthropy. A woman can choose self-owned business as her career choice provided she is to ready to face the challenges that lie ahead of her, ready to walk the extra mile and ready to rely on her own vast resources and abilities.

Conclusion

Independence brought promise of equality of opportunity in all sphere to the Indian women and laws guaranteeing for their equal rights of participation in political process and equal opportunities and rights in education and employment were enacted. But unfortunately, the government sponsored development activities have benefited only a small section of women. The large majority of them are still unaffected by change and development activities have benefited only a small section of women i.e. the urban middle class women. The large majority of them are still unaffected by change and development. The reasons are well sighted in the discussion part of this article. It is hoped that the suggestions forwarded in the article will help the entrepreneurs in particular and policy-planners in general to look into this problem and develop better schemes, developmental programmes and opportunities to the women folk to enter into more entrepreneurial ventures.

References

1. Boserup, Ester , *Women's Role in Economic Development'* George Allen and Unwin 1970, London.

2. Ajit Chose " Current Issues of Employment in India", *EPW*, Vol. 34 No. 36, 4th September, 1999.

3. Padma, *Women Workers in India in the 21st Century- Unemployment and Underemployment*: www.cpiml. ICI.org, 2004

4. S. Rothbock, *et.al*, Labour in the New Economy-2001.

5. Padma, "Women Workers in India in the 21st Century- Unemployment and Underemployment: www.cpiml. ICI.org, 2004

6. Meena, N.L. (1991), 'National Policy and Programmes for Women in India' in *Papers and Proceedings of the Regional Conference on Gender Issues in Agriculture*, ADB and UNIFEM. (Manila, 5-6 December, 1990).

7. Jose p., Ajith Kumar and Paul T.M. (1994), *Entrepreneurship Development*, Himalaya Publishing.

8. Starcher, D.C. (1996), Women Entrepreneurs: Catalysts for Transformation. July 6, 2001: http://www.ebbf.org/woman. htm'O (c2001269511).

9. "The Female Poverty Trap" (2001, May 8), The Economist, Retrieved March 14, 2001: http.//www economist com.

10. Amarnath, Nischinta; Ghosh, Debashjsh (2005). The Voyage to Excellence: The Ascent of 21 Women Leaders of India Inc., Pustak Mahal.

11. Robbins, P. Stephens (1999), Organisational Behaviour —Concepts, Controversies, Applications, Prentice Hall of India Private Limited,: 8th Edition.

12. Sekharan, Uma (2004), Organisational Behavior—Text and Cases, TataMcGraw-Hill Publishing Company Limited, New Delhi, 2-Edition.

Women Entrepreneurship
Indian Perspective

Dr. Prfulla Ch. Mohapatra
Mr. Jaba Varadwaj

"Nobody talks of women entrepreneurship as survival, but that's exactly what it is today"

—Anita Roddick

ABSTRACT

Development of entrepreneurship in general and women entrepreneurship in particular is emphasized by most of the countries of the world from the points of view of promising benefits of generating ample employment opportunities, increasing productivity, creating new technologies, products and services and all in all accelerating overall economic growth of a nation. In the Indian context, promotion of women entrepreneurship has become an imperative not because it encourages women to have an independent occupation but because it helps them to stand on their own legs. Besides, women entrepreneurs learn to explore the prospects of starting new enterprise, undertake risks; to acquire skill of introduction of new innovations, co-ordination, administration and control of business and providing effective leadership.

The present chapter is an exercise focussing on some of the key aspects concerning starting and growing in entrepreneurship with special emphasis on women entrepreneurship in Indian perspective. The discussion covers the required skills of a successful entrepreneur highlighting on knowledge-training, required competencies, development needs of women entrepreneur- managers, personality types etc. In addition, problems of women entrepreneurs in India with right efforts required in mitigating them have also been a part of the discussion.

Introduction

Development of entrepreneurship not only generates ample opportunities for self-employment but also it makes significant contributions for fostering economic growth, increasing productivity and creating new technologies, products and services.

Entrepreneurship is defined as the "practice of starting new organizations or revitalizing mature organizations, generally in response to identified opportunities". In Mariam Webster, an entrepreneur is defined as the " one who organizes, manages, and assumes the risks of a business or enterprise" Entrepreneurship is often a difficult undertaking as a vast majority of new businesses fail. Entrepreneurial activities are substantially different depending on the type of organization that is being started. It ranges in scale from solo projects (even involving the entrepreneur only part-time) to major undertakings creating many job opportunities. For women in India, entrepreneurship today is a question of empowerment and survival. Therefore, it is more relevant to help them grow in small entrepreneurial management so that large numbers of women flood into business activities and bring out revolutionary change in the field of business and enterprise in India.

Here is an attempt to discuss some of the important aspects that need careful consideration for promoting entrepreneurship in general and women entrepreneurship in particular in the Indian perspective.

Conceptual Sagnificance

***Mary Kay Ash**, founder of Mary Kay Cosmetics on her address to women entrepreneurs attending the Geneva Summit (2008) said, "When you reach an obstacle, turn it into an opportunity. You have the choice. You can overcome and be a winner, or you can allow it to overcome you and be a loser. The choice is yours and yours alone. Go that extra mile that failures refuse to travel. It is far better to be exhausted from success than to be rested from failure."*

Starting and growing in entrepreneurship requires many skills to be successful, which can be called a business personality. It includes those traits and characteristics of a person that blend with the needs of the business. When a person better understands and integrates his business personality, then he can give his best part to the success of the enterprise. Compared to men, women lag behind in entrepreneurial personality traits because of the traditional male dominance in business enterprise, negative social perception about women in business, lack of business knowledge, proper training and motivational encouragement, and finally for the burden of child rearing responsibilities. However, it is reported in several research studies that women are in no way inferior to men with respect to the 9 core structure personality traits of 'Enneagram' (Figure 10.1); rather in some of the traits like enthusiasm, achievement motivation, and loyalty, women are better than men. Such findings point to the fact that given appropriate opportunities for training and development in business attitude, knowledge, motivation and personality, women would scale high on men in entrepreneurship.

There are many theories and views on what makes a person an entrepreneur. At one extreme is the view that an entrepreneur is born already endowed with the entrepreneurial traits of enterprise and business acumen. At the other end is the view that any person can become an entrepreneur when placed (or forced) in a situation which provides the opportunities (or requires) for the practice of entrepreneurship. The experience and studies during the past

Fig. 10.1: **Enneagram: The Core Business Personality Traits**

40 years of active entrepreneurship and small enterprise development promotion show that in reality, the development of entrepreneurial traits and behavior is somewhere in between these extremes, leading to widespread practices of entrepreneurship education, training and development and the creation of conducive and enabling environment for the start-up and growth of enterprises.

Entrepreneurship *vs.* Small Scale Enterprises

Entrepreneurship development was considered as one of the important objectives of promoting small scale industries not only in India but also all over the world. Small enterprises, therefore, are closely linked with the practice of entrepreneurship and where the strategic and operational management decision making primarily rests with one or two persons who, most often than not, is/are owner(s) of the enterprise. The independence of the small enterprise is also a criterion, i.e. not being a subsidiary or production unit of a larger firm. Small enterprises, although very often referred to as a sector in business development literature, are very heterogeneous. While some generalizations can be made concerning the characteristics of small enterprises, it is best to keep in mind that small enterprises vary in size, in the type of business they are engaged in, in the industry sector they are operating in, in the products and services produced, in the processes and level of technology used, in the specific community and business environment where they are located, etc. Thus, in addition to generic competencies, there will be particular capabilities, knowledge and skills that will be required of the entrepreneur-manager based on the specific characteristics of his or her small business.

There is a close and intimate identification between the entrepreneur-manager and his or her small business. The development of the competencies of entrepreneur-manager is closely linked to the development of the small business and the development of the business invariably requires the development of the competencies of the entrepreneur-managers. This very close identification of the person and the business leads to particular and specific nature of the resulting management style, systems and practices in the small business. Different stages in the life cycle of the enterprise require specific competencies and capabilities of the entrepreneur manager which must be considered in formulating and implementing training and development interventions.

The effective training and development of entrepreneur-managers requires particular competencies from the trainers and those who are organizing the programme. Not only must they have the technical knowledge and abilities, but they must also have the attitudinal, behavioral and personal competencies that will enable them to deliver the program and the specific training intervention in such manner suitable to the learning process and preferences of the target group. In general, the training and development programme will consist of not just one standard, structured training intervention but will be made up of combinations of training and development approaches which are flexible and can be modified as the programme progresses.

Basic Requirements

As development of women entrepreneurship in India has become a necessity following are some of the areas that require special attention and consideration:

Knowledge Training: Entrepreneur-managers of small enterprises perform two distinct yet closely intertwined functions: entrepreneurship and management. These functions are so embedded in each other that it is very difficult in practice to deal effectively with each of the functions. Entrepreneurs need to be provided with knowledge about various aspects of entrepreneurship such as personality profile about good entrepreneurship (Table 10.1).

Table 10.1: Profile of an Entrepreneur

Characteristic	Traits
Self-confidence	Belief in own ability Independence Optimism
Strong will power	Persistence and perseverance, Determination
Task/result-oriented	Achievement oriented hard work, drive, energy, initiative
Risk-taker	Risk assessment and judicious risk taking ability Likes challenges
Leadership	Good communicator gets along well with others responsive to suggestions, criticism, concern for other persons develops other people
Originality	Innovative, creative, flexible (open minded), resourceful versatile, knowledgeable
Future-oriented	Foresight, vision, perceptiveness

Required Competencies: Entrepreneurs, being persons having internal locus of control (Ward, 1993), provide the driving force behind the small businesses based on their belief that their behaviour and action, rather than outside factors beyond their control, determine the outcome of any endeavour. They believe that environmental factors and their changes can be influenced and managed for business development. These beliefs are the source of the self-confidence in their exercise of the leadership of the small business. They provide the insight and the vision, being perceptually alert and having high ability to see opportunities and threats in the environment. This ability to recognize business opportunities and develop them makes them the source of innovations in products and services, in new processes and work organization, in marketing and distribution, in business practices—of the enterprise. The entrepreneur provides the links of the small business to its environment, relying on informal and formal networks of family members, friends and business people for information, support and resources essential to the start-up and running of the small business. These networks of individuals and businesses are vital to perceive opportunities, test ideas, acquire information and knowledge on best practices, and mobilize resources to create the new enterprise. They help the entrepreneur and the small business keep abreast of current trends, get to know of new technologies, assess changing customer trends and develop new ways to manage and solve problems (Tjosvold and Weicker, 1993). The competencies required to perform these entrepreneurial functions effectively are:

- *Perceptiveness:* The ability to be alert for and identify new business opportunities;
- *Analytical ability:* The ability to analyze an opportunity or a problem situation, to be able to look at the situation holistically and to break it down into components allowing the analysis of cause and effects and other relationships;
- *Decision-making:* Identification and evaluation of alternatives and selection of what appears to be the best solution or course of action to take;
- *Learning ability:* The ability to derive lessons and insights from experiences and to apply these learning to other situations;

- *Initiative:* The ability to be self-driven and motivated and to keep on going without waiting to be told to do so by others;
- *Empathy:* The ability to identify oneself mentally with customers, clients, suppliers, competitors, service providers and other stakeholders in the business environment thus comprehending better their needs, expectations, apprehensions and requirements;
- *Persuasion:* The ability to communicate with others (customers, suppliers, partners, workers, government officials, etc.), make them understand and convince them on a particular proposition;
- *Negotiating ability:* The ability to discuss the various sides of an issue or proposal and strike agreements that are mutually advantageous and acceptable to all parties involved;
- *Networking:* The ability to establish linkages with other business persons and other stakeholders for mutual learning, collaborative undertakings and other joint activities aimed at achieving common objectives.

While these abilities are developed and honed through practice and experiences, they could also be developed by proper training e.g. through training approaches that provide opportunities for exercises and practice in business environmental scanning and analysis, market opportunity identification, creativity and innovation, problem solving techniques, communication, persuasion and negotiation and actually going through the various phases of starting the business.

Development Needs of Women Entrepreneurs — Managers

The knowledge, attitudes and skills needed by the women entrepreneur-manager will vary at different stages in the life of her small business. The competencies required to conceive and start a small business will be different from those needed to make the enterprise survive, be profitable and grow. At the stage where the business is transforming from small to a medium enterprise, the attitudes, management style and competencies required will be totally different.

The development needs of women entrepreneur-managers alongside the enterprise development phases are discussed in the following order as:

- Conducive and enabling environment;
- Awareness and Pre-start-up Preparation;
- Business Start-up;
- Survival and Strengthening;
- Growth and Expansion.

Conducive and Enabling Environment

The capability building of entrepreneur-managers starts with the creation of a conducive and enabling environment for small business creation and development. Such an environment not only encourages the start-up of new business and nurtures its development, but it also provides the learning environment, stimuli and opportunities for entrepreneur-managers to continuously pursue, at all stages in the development of their small businesses, self-development and enhancement of their capabilities.

It is now widely recognized that a conducive and enabling environment is crucial to the development of small enterprises (Tolentino, 1995). The over-all macro and micro economic framework, the legal and regulatory environment as well as political climate influence the rate of new business creation and their survival and growth. A healthy economic and business climate based on market principles is of critical importance for a growing and dynamic small enterprise sector. Small enterprises are, after all, just like any other participants in the economic life of a country. They will develop when the over-all environment is favorable to the growth of the whole economy. Creating an enabling environment for the development of the small enterprise sector therefore implies first of all the creation of a favorable overall policy framework for the development of all enterprises and of entrepreneurship. Such an environment must provide the possible rewards and gains for potential entrepreneurs to venture into private business, market opportunities for business viability, and a policy and regulatory regime that makes it easy for people to start and operate a business and that offers a 'level playing field' to enterprises of all sizes.

Small enterprises, because of their sizes and particular characteristics discussed earlier, have certain constraints that may require them to seek assistance and support from outside sources. They are also often subject to policies and incentive schemes that are biased towards the large enterprises. To offset these disadvantages, small enterprise promotional programs and support schemes are often necessary and the setting-up and strengthening of the supportive institutional framework (governmental as well as private) is required. These support programmes and institutions provide, on need basis, services that help and build the capabilities of the entrepreneur-managers to deal with specific business concerns such as access to markets, development of internal management systems, improving productivity, technology upgrading, etc.

The formation of the entrepreneur-manager starts with the 'enterprise culture' of the person's immediate family and community and society at large. Entrepreneurship is a behavioural pattern shaped by the attitude of society towards business and nurtured by a 'culture' that values and regards highly success in business. This 'enterprise culture' sees entrepreneurship as a desired way of achieving economic, social and political success and provides the social, financial, and technical and market support networks that facilitate people's entry into and conduct of business. Young people growing-up in this culture are exposed and immersed in business operations in their formative years. Their attitudes and predisposition to entrepreneurship are shaped and reinforced by:

(a) Abundant role models and positive images of successful business persons and those who 'made well' in business;

(b) A community value system that puts success in business and enterprising behaviour in high esteem, thereby providing societal recognition and positive encouragement to the practice of entrepreneurship;

(c) Ample opportunity for familiarization (even when still very young) with small business tasks through involvement in entrepreneurial activities of the family or the community *e.g.* through helping in the family's business or through formal or informal apprenticeship in small businesses;

(d) A network of business and family contacts that provide a learning support environment to young people venturing into business *e.g.* bankers providing advice on financial management, suppliers that assist in the development of good supply chain management, clients and customers providing marketing information and advice, regulatory agencies that provide good information and extend assistance in meeting the requirements of the legal and regulatory system, industry associations providing linkages and extended networking, etc. and

(e) A business community that helps young people with business entry opportunities and provides some "incubation" support *e.g.* providing initial market opportunity, access to soft financing, trade credits and consignments, management and technical advice, etc.

In a community or society where this opportunity for young people to be exposed to the practice of entrepreneurship and to the actual operations business is limited, entrepreneurship education and education for enterprise programmes are being incorporated in the educational system. Many of these programs introduce entrepreneurship exposure and basic business training at the secondary and tertiary education levels. In order to really simulate and try to duplicate the effects of enterprise culture however, it is important to already introduce in the early stages of the education system (even at kindergarten and pre-school stage) the learning materials, teaching methodologies and learning activities that develop in the children enterprising behaviour and attributes. Using forms and media appropriate to the age levels, children could already be provided, through curricular and extracurricular exercises, orientation on how to integrate human, financial, material and technical resources in their environment to solve problems and achieve goals by means of competition and cooperation, teamwork and use of mutual learning.

Awareness and Pre-start-up

Small enterprise is created through a process that brings together human potential and environmental potential into a business undertaking. The human potential (for example, entrepreneurship, managerial and technical competency) combines with the environmental potential (which includes real market opportunities, availability of inputs, technology, capital, encouraging policy, etc.) resulting into a value-creating and profit-making enterprise. The process leading to a successful small business is triggered, initiated and pursued by the entrepreneur who perceives the opportunity, thinks of a business idea to take advantage of the opportunity and mobilizes the necessary resources to bring his venture into reality.

At this stage in the development of the business, the training and development of the potential entrepreneur should be aimed at:

(a) Developing entrepreneurial skills, behaviour and attributes;

(b) Developing self-awareness of one's own predisposition and capability for setting-up and running a business;

(c) Developing real insights into the business development process, its rewards, demands, pitfalls, and competency requirements; and

(*d*) Expanding exposures to business world to sharpen business opportunity identification capabilities.

An example of a pre-start-up training addressed to youth is the Know About Business (KAB) of the ILO International Training Centre in Turin (Box 1). The purpose of the KAB is not necessarily to have young people begin their careers immediately as entrepreneurs or self-employed people. Rather it is to give them awareness and some practice of the opportunities, challenges, procedures, characteristics, attitudes and skills needed for entrepreneurship and self-employment (Manu, 1996). The specific training and development interventions to achieve these preparations towards venturing into business will be dictated by the needs and requirements of particular target groups *e.g.* displaced workers, retirees, women, unemployed graduates, and youth in their formative years. For example, the issues addressed by the education program for preparing women for entrepreneurship are as shown in Box below:

BOX 10.1
KNOW ABOUT BUSINESS

Know about business (KAB) training package seeks to develop entrepreneurial skills and in the process prepare participants not only to establish their own businesses in the future but also to work productively in small and medium enterprises. The package is designed for use by trainers/teachers in vocational and technical training institutions. It consists of a Trainer Handbook and 8 learning modules. Each module presents a key area of entrepreneurship and is divided in several topics. Furthermore, each module is designed as a stand-alone package, requiring no previous knowledge of the others. The titles of the modules are in the form of questions, the answers to which the trainees should know at the completion of the module.

Trainer Handbook

- What is the background and general aim of the KAB?

- Why is entrepreneurship education important?
- Scope of enterprise
- Objectives of KAB
- Target group and beneficiaries of KAB
- Modules, contents, formats and duration of KAB
- How and who to teach KAB
- Training methodology of KAB
- Gender considerations

Module 1: What is enterprise?

- Meaning and scope of enterprise
- Different forms of enterprise
- Roles people play in enterprise
- Small enterprise

Module 2: Why entrepreneurship?

- Entrepreneurship meaning
- Reasons for entrepreneurship in business
- Importance of entrepreneurship in society
- Self-employment

Module 3: Who are entrepreneurs?

- Assessing entrepreneurial potential
- Identifying entrepreneurial characteristics
- Entrepreneurs as leaders
- Entrepreneurial decision making
- Risk-taking

Module 4: How do I become an entrepreneur?

- Competencies for successful entrepreneurship
- Key success factors in setting-up a small business
- The entrepreneurial decision

Module 5: How do I find a good business idea?

- Generating ideas
- Identifying and assessing business opportunities

Module 6: How do I organize and enterprise

- Potential problems in starting an enterprise
- Selecting a suitable market
- Legal forms of business ownership
- Obtaining money to start an enterprise
- Buying or starting a business
- Selecting a business location
- Selecting suppliers

Module 7: How do I operate the enterprise?

- Hiring and managing people
- Managing money
- use of financial statements
- Small business technology
- Managing sales

Module 8: What are the next steps to become an entrepreneur

- Sources of further assistance
- Preparing a business plan
- Being involved in an enterprise
- Maintaining entrepreneurial outlook

Business Start-up

At this stage, the potential entrepreneur validates and refines his or her business ideas, and makes the decision whether to undertake or not the particular business venture being considered. What is really involved is a series of decision-making process where initial and tentative decisions are made on target markets, products and services, business forms and business strategies. The appropriateness of these tentative decisions are then tested in the market place through research and sometimes test marketing. New decisions are made based on findings and results, and the cycle is repeated until some confidence is reached on the viability of the business idea. Depending again on the size and complexity of the business being conceived, such decision making process could take a very short time or it could be involved and intensive. If the final decision is go, resources and linkages are mobilized to set-up the business. At various phases of this iterative analysis-decision-action process, the entrepreneur-manager requires specific competencies and capabilities. The training and development needs often involves reinforcement of the entrepreneurial attributes, acquiring basic knowledge of business systems and of how to manage a small business, developing business contacts and linkages *i.e.* the 'know who', and development of skills for preparing, analyzing and evaluating business plans. In the choice of particular training and development interventions to be used in this stage the following issues must be considered and fully appreciated (Kubr and Prokopenko, 1989).

- The particular target group, their characteristics and needs. Small business entrepreneurship and start-up training are usually done with a specific target group e.g. unemployed youth, educated unemployed, women, workers that became redundant, retired workers, etc. Each specific target group has particular characteristics, capabilities, constraints and needs that must be taken into considerations in the design and delivery of the training activities.
- The potential entrepreneurs and founders of new small businesses come from various social environments which may lack the opportunity for business experience and enterprise culture discussed earlier.
- The persons concerned may have very different individual backgrounds as regards to education,

technical skills, practical experience, family circumstances, etc.

- The standards to be achieved are very difficult to establish since they depend on a number of factors and forces influencing the development of business in the given country environment.
- In addition, many different views exist on whether and how training can help potential and new entrepreneur; the different conceptual approaches to training and non-training interventions have considerable influence on all stages of training program design and delivery.

One mistake often made is to front-load the training programs, aiming to impart the maximum possible knowledge and skills even before the business creation process starts. As a result, the amount of knowledge provided exceeds the knowledge actually needed in the various stages of the start-up process and the instruction remains essentially theoretical. Motivation and reinforcement through practical applications are missing. On the other hand, the programme graduates will inevitably encounter numerous problems which were ignored or not anticipated in a generalized course.

To avoid such pitfall, practitioners of entrepreneurship development suggest that training programs and strategies be such that training is related to competency needs as they occur during the business-start-up process and that the learning situations that come-up while solving problems and difficulties encountered at various stages be exploited and maximized as capability building opportunities. In this approach, some basic and introductory training on business start-up and small business management are given at the start of the programme. The participants then embark on the iterative processes involved in starting a business discussed above. The potential entrepreneur learns by doing as he or she goes through the various steps of setting-up the business. This approach makes it possible to discriminate effectively between common training needs of all programme participants which can be met through courses, workshops, group discussions, and briefing sessions before and during the formal training program, and individual needs which can be met in several ways (special course, self-study, action learning, counselling, etc.) at the appropriate points of the enterprise creation process. This will also allow the effective use of a combination of training and non-training intervention and assistance to the potential entrepreneur. Training can be made to fit individual learning needs and the pace of learning which a participant is able to follow. Furthermore, training can be better focussed not only on the profile of a particular individual, but simultaneously on needs related to his or her specific business idea and project. The link between the concepts and techniques to real business situation is also highlighted, leading to enhanced learning motivation and retention.

However, before adopting this pattern of tailor-made and action-oriented training, it is necessary to ascertain its feasibility from the viewpoint of time, costs, and the competence and flexibility requirements on trainers and counselors. Generally speaking, the trainers' experiences and competencies are very important factors affecting the design of a training and assistance programme. In many cases it will be a limiting factor: a program that is too demanding on methodology, and on the trainers' time and experience, will have to be simplified to be realistic.

Survival and Strengthening

Setting-up a business is one thing and making it viable and profitable is another thing. In fact, small business mortality is very high during the first and second year of its operations. This is the period where the entrepreneur-manager must fully apply his or her entrepreneurial and managerial competencies to make the business competitive and profitable. It is also the period of maximum learning. The basic skills acquired from the start-up stage and the rudimentary business systems installed at the time the business was created are not sufficient to insure the successful running of the small enterprise. New or enhanced competencies are needed to improve the various systems (marketing, production, finance, personnel, etc.) as well as quality and productivity. Processes will need refinement and upgrading. New 'know-how and know-who' linkages must be established and managed. In addition to the above, the managerial competencies of the entrepreneur must be developed and honed-up in the following areas:

- One very important managerial skill that is needed to be acquired and honed-up right at the early stages in the life of the enterprise is cash flow management. Small enterprises, with its limited resources, even though they have excellent market opportunities, good and distinctive products and technologies, skilled and capable workers could still fail due to lack of liquidity because of poor cash flow management.
- Another competence that will be required to be upgraded is productivity and quality management. The competitiveness of enterprises now are getting to be more and more based on product and service quality and timely delivery performance. This is particularly true for those who are sub-contractors and suppliers in a bigger production network.
- Competence in the use and application of computers and electronic communications is also getting to be essential. The cost of computer hardware is continuously decreasing and there is a wealth of business software applications that would be very useful in managing small businesses. More and more, information on market developments and technical advance are provided through electronic data bases and information services. Business communications and transactions are increasingly done by e-mail and other means through the Interent. In the area of marketing and distribution, it is expected that electronic marketing will be a growth area for small businesses.

Again, the training and development interventions must be suited to the learning needs and learning capacity of the entrepreneur-managers. In addition to standard short courses on functional areas such as general management, marketing and sales, financial management, and production management, training and non-training intervention must be provided addressing the entrepreneurs-managers' need for information on the business environment, further development of problem solving, communicating, leading, negotiating, and other 'soft skills', and for dealing with problems and concerns specific to the industry sector where the small business is.

In some cases, training and development interventions are needed because of current weaknesses and difficulties being experienced by the small enterprise. In this particular situation, a good problem identification and improvement needs diagnosis (using some of the techniques described in Appendix 2 and other consulting tools) is required. The diagnosis will often uncover both training and non-training needs-related causes of the weakness or difficulties for which appropriate training and non-training interventions would be required. For example, the problem of lack of liquidity could be addressed by training the entrepreneur manager in cash flow management, purchasing and stock control, credit management, etc. and by linking with sources of short term financing, trade credits and working capital.

Entrepreneur-managers of small businesses have been found to tap more their network of family members, associates, competitors, customers, suppliers and other business counterparts to learn and obtain needed information. Such sources of learning should be encouraged and utilized. In particular, learning from the experiences of other entrepreneur-managers (both of those in the same business sector and those in other trades) must be maximized. In addition to structured formal exchange of experiences (e.g having an experienced business person present his or her experiences in a classroom training situation) study visits, business clinics, action learning, bench marking, etc. could be explored. Joint programs with industry associations, chambers of industry and commerce, and other trade groupings should be availed of to catalyze and facilitate this peer learning process. The formation of business networks and clusters to exchange ideas, information and experiences should be promoted and encouraged.

Growth and Expansion

This stage requires completely new competencies of the entrepreneur-manager. Enterprise growth could involve any or all of the following: increase in size in terms of volume of business and employment, increased diversity of product types and product lines, expansion into new markets whether domestic or foreign, adoption of new processes and higher technology (Tolentino and Theocharides, 1992). Correspondingly, new and better management systems must be installed, increased decentralization, delegation and specialization in functional decision-making is called for, and strategic matters will concern more the entrepreneur-manager. The small business transforms itself into a medium enterprise.

The middle managers and supervisors who are assuming more managerial functions in the areas of marketing, finance, production, personnel, etc. will require the build-up of their competencies in these areas. Providing short courses on these functional areas of management will therefore help in building the competency base and the managerial talent pool of small enterprises, enabling them to go through the transition process.

The patterns of relationships within the enterprise also change. Communications and interactions with workers and supervisors that used to be direct, informal and personal become more structured and formal. The ability to maintain good labor-management relations and good relations among the employees of the enterprise is now even more important. At this stage in the life of the business, human and social capital development in the form of good interpersonal relations, mutual respect and trust, sense of community and belonging, cooperation and team spirit, etc. become very critical for the enterprise's continued growth and development, even to its surviving the internal stresses of the transition process.

As business grows, having good internal (vertical and horizontal) and external communication with customers, distributors, retailers, suppliers, banks, government agencies and local community become critically important for increased understanding, cooperation and mutual thrust. Whereas before, with the smaller size of the business, the entrepreneur-manager could devote personal time and attention to these important relationships with the internal and external stakeholders, as the size and complexity of the business increases the responsibility for contacts and maintaining good communication and relations must now be shared with the other key managers and personnel of the enterprise.

Training and development programmes that help the entrepreneur-managers to be aware and understand the transformations (their own as well as of their businesses) required will go a long way in preparing them emotionally, behaviourally and technically for the change process. Equipping them with skills in analysing the strong and weak points of their enterprises as well as of the threats and opportunities in the business environment, and developing competencies related to strategic corporate planning well also be useful. Interventions aimed at developing the new managerial skills required by the new forms of enterprises and work organizations such as facilitating, negotiating, team building, networking will help them prepare for the top management roles in a medium or large enterprise that their businesses have become. Growth programs developed originally in UK and aimed at small enterprises with growth potential addresses some or most of these training needs. An example of a training programme that addresses many of these needs is the Small Firms Growth Programme of the Small Business Centre of Durham University Business School (DUBS, 1991).

The 9 Personality types of Entrepreneurs

1. *The Improver:* If one operates his business predominately in the improver mode, he is focused on using his company as a means to improve the world. His overarching motto is, 'morally correct companies will be rewarded working on a noble cause'. Improvers have an unwavering ability to run their business with high integrity and ethics. However, its Personality Alert is to be aware of the tendency to be a perfectionist and over-critical of employees and customers. The exemplar of this entrepreneur personality is Anita Roddick, founder of The Body Shop.
2. *The Advisor:* This business personality type provides an extremely high level of assistance and advice to customers. The advisor's motto is, 'the customer is right and we must do everything to please him'. Companies built by advisors become customer focused. The Personality Alert for Advisors is that they may become totally focussed on the needs of their business and customers because of which they may ignore their own needs and ultimately burn out. John W. Nordstrom, Founder Nordstrom is the best example of such an entrepreneur.
3. *The Superstar:* Here the business is centered on the charisma and high energy of the Superstar CEO. This personality often will cause to build his business around his own personal brand. His Personality Alert is that he may be too competitive and workaholic. Donald Trump, CEO of Trump Hotels and Casino Resorts is an example of superstar entrepreneur.
4. *The Artist* This business personality is the reserved but highly creative type who is often found in businesses demanding creativity such as web design and ad

agencies. As an artist type he tends to build his business around the unique talents and creativities he has. The Personality Alert for the artist entrepreneur is that he may be overly sensitive to his customer's responses even if the feedback is constructive that leads to a negative self-image. Scott Adams, Creator of Dilbert is an example of artist entrepreneur.

5. ***The Visionary:*** A business built by a Visionary will often be based on the future vision and thoughts of the founder. He will have a high degree of curiosity to understand the world around him and will set-up plans to avoid the landmines. Personality Alert is that visionaries can be too focussed on the dream with little focus on reality leading to action that precedes vision. Bill Gates, Founder of Micro Soft Inc. is the example of visionary entrepreneur.

6. ***The Analyst:*** If you run a business as an Analyst, your company is focused on fixing problems in a systematic way. Often the basis for science, engineering or computer firms, Analyst companies excel at problem solving. Personality Alert: Be aware of analysis paralysis. Work on trusting others. Entrepreneurial example: Intel Founder, Gordon Moore.

7. ***The Fireball:*** A business owned and operated by a Fireball is full of life, energy and optimism. Your company is life-energizing and makes customers feel the company has a get it done attitude in a fun playful manner. Personality Alert: You may over commit your teams and act to impulsively. Balance your impulsiveness with business planning. Entrepreneurial example: Malcolm Forbes, Publisher, Forbes Magazine.

8. ***The Hero:*** You have an incredible will and ability to lead the world and your business through any challenge. You are the essence of entrepreneurship and can assemble great companies.

   Personality Alert: Over promising and using force full tactics to get your way will not work long term. To be successful, trust your leadership skills to help others find their way. Entrepreneurial example: Jack Welch, CEO GE.

9. ***The Healer:*** If you are a Healer, you provide nurturing and harmony to your business. You have an uncanny ability to survive and persist with an inner calm. *Personality Alert:* Because of your caring, healing attitude toward your business, you may avoid outside realities and use wishful thinking. Use scenario planning to prepare for turmoil. *Entrepreneurial example:* Ben Cohen, Co-Founder of Ben and Jerry's Ice Cream.

Each business personality type can succeed in the business environment if you stay true to your character. Knowing firmly what your strong traits are can act as a compass for your small business. If you are building a team, this insight is invaluable. For the solo business owners, understand that you may need outside help to balance your business personality.

If one has got many or all of these traits, one's entrepreneurial success is more promising:

- ***An eye for opportunity:*** Many entrepreneurs start by finding a need and quickly satisfying it.
- ***Independence:*** Even though most entrepreneurs know how to work within the framework for the sake of profits, they enjoy being their own boss.
- ***An appetite for hard work:*** Most entrepreneurs start out working long, hard hours with little pay.
- ***Self-confidence:*** Entrepreneurs must demonstrate extreme self-confidence in order to cope with all the risks of operating their own business.
- ***Discipline:*** Successful entrepreneurs resist the temptation to do what is unimportant or the easiest but have the ability to think through to what is the most essential.

- *Judgement:* Successful entrepreneurs have the ability to think quickly and make a wise decision.
- *Ability to accept change:* Change occurs frequently when you own your own business, the entrepreneur thrives on changes and their businesses grow.
- *Make stress work for them:* On the roller coaster to business success the entrepreneur often copes by focusing on the end result and not the process of getting there.
- *Need to achieve:* Although they keep an "eye" on profits, this is often secondary to the drive toward personal success.
- *Focus on profits:* Successful entrepreneurs always have the profit margin in sight and know that their business success is measured by profits. Is this your profile or would you rather do your job, pick up your paycheck and leave the headaches to someone else? Most of us, quite easily, choose the later.

Push-pull Factors and Women in Business

Women Entrepreneurs may be defined as the women or a group of women who initiate, organize and operate a business enterprise. Government of India has defined women entrepreneurs as an enterprise owned and controlled by a women having a minimum financial interest of 51 per cent of the capital and giving at least 51 per cent of employment generated in the enterprise to women. Like a male entrepreneur, a woman entrepreneur has many functions. They should explore the prospects of starting new enterprise; undertake risks, introduction of new innovations, coordination administration and control of business and providing effective leadership in all aspects of business.

Women in business are a recent phenomenon in India. By and large they had confide themselves to petty business and tiny cottage industries. Women entrepreneurs engaged in business due to push and pull factors which encourage women to have an independent occupation and stand on their own legs. A sense towards independent decision-making on their life and career is the motivational factor behind this urge. Saddled with household chores and domestic responsibilities women want to get independence under the influence of these factors the women entrepreneurs choose a profession as a challenge and as an urge to do some thing new. Such situation is described as pull factors. While in push factors women engaged in business activities due to family compulsion and the responsibility is thrust upon them.

Problems of Women Entrepreneurs in India

Women in India are faced many problems to get ahead their life in business. A few problems cane be detailed as:

1. *The greatest deterrent to women entrepreneurs is that they are women:* A kind of patriarchal – male dominant social order is the building block to them in their way towards business success. Male members think it a big risk financing the ventures run by women.

2. *The financial institutions are skeptical about the entrepreneurial abilities of women:* The bankers consider women loonies as higher risk than men loonies. The bankers put unrealistic and unreasonable securities to get loan to women entrepreneurs. According to a report by the United Nations Industrial Development Organization (UNIDO), "despite evidence that woman's loan repayment rates are higher than men's, women still face more difficulties in obtaining credit," often due to discriminatory attitudes of banks and informal lending groups (UNIDO, 1995b).

3. Entrepreneurs usually require financial assistance of some kind to launch their ventures — be it a formal bank loan or money from a savings account. Women in developing nations have little access to funds, due to the fact that they are concentrated in poor rural communities with few opportunities to borrow money (Starcher, 1996; UNIDO, 1995a). The women entrepreneurs are suffering from inadequate financial resources and working capital.

The women entrepreneurs lack access to external funds due to their inability to provide tangible security. Very few women have the tangible property in hand.

4. *Women's family obligations also bar them from becoming successful entrepreneurs in both developed and developing nations.* "Having primary responsibility for children, home and older dependent family members, few women can devote all their time and energies to their business" (Starcher, 1996, p. 8). The financial institutions discourage women entrepreneurs on the belief that they can at any time leave their business and become housewives again. The result is that they are forced to rely on their own savings, and loan from relatives and family friends.

5. *Indian women give more emphasis to family ties and relationships.* Married women have to make a fine balance between business and home. More over the business success is depends on the support the family members extended to women in the business process and management. The interest of the family members is a determinant factor in the realization of women folk business aspirations.

6. *Another argument is that women entrepreneurs have low-level management skills.* They have to depend on office staffs and intermediaries, to get things done, especially, the marketing and sales side of business. Here there is more probability for business fallacies like the intermediaries take major part of the surplus or profit. Marketing means mobility and confidence in dealing with the external world, both of which women have been discouraged from developing by social conditioning. Even when they are otherwise in control of an enterprise, they often depend on males of the family in this area.

7. *The male-female competition is another factor,* which develop hurdles to women entrepreneurs in the business management process. Despite the fact that women entrepreneurs are good in keeping their service prompt and delivery in time, due to lack of organizational skills

compared to male entrepreneurs women have to face constraints from competition. The confidence to travel across day and night and even different regions and states are less found in women compared to male entrepreneurs. This shows the low level freedom of expression and freedom of mobility of the women entrepreneurs.

8. *Knowledge of alternative source of raw materials availability and high negotiation skills are the basic requirement to run a business*. Getting the raw materials from different souse with discount prices is the factor that determines the profit margin. Lack of knowledge of availability of the raw materials and low-level negotiation and bargaining skills are the factors, which affect women entrepreneur's business adventures.

9. *Knowledge of latest technological changes, know how, and education level of the person are significant factor that affect business*. The literacy rate of women in India is found at low level compared to male population. Many women in developing nations lack the education needed to spur successful entrepreneurship. They are ignorant of new technologies or unskilled in their use, and often unable to do research and gain the necessary training (UNIDO, 1995b, p. 1). Although great advances are being made in technology, many women's illiteracy, structural difficulties, and lack of access to technical training prevent the technology from being beneficial or even available to females ("Women Entrepreneurs in Poorest Countries," 2001). According to The Economist, this lack of knowledge and the continuing treatment of women as second-class citizens keep them in a pervasive cycle of poverty ("The Female Poverty Trap," 2001). The studies indicate that uneducated women don't have the knowledge of measurement and basic accounting.

10. *Low-level risk taking attitude is another factor affecting women folk decision to get into business*. Low-level education provides low-level self-confidence and self-reliance to

the women folk to engage in business, which is continuous risk taking and strategic cession making profession. Investing money, maintaining the operations and ploughing back money for surplus generation requires high risk taking attitude, courage and confidence. Though the risk tolerance ability of the women-folk in day-to-day life is high compared to male members, while in business it is found opposite to that.

11. Achievement motivation of the women-folk found less compared to male members. The low level of education and confidence leads to low level achievement and advancement motivation among women folk to engage in business operations and running a business concern.
12. Finally high production cost of some business operations adversely affects the development of women entrepreneurs. The installation of new machineries during expansion of the productive capacity and like similar factors dissuades the women entrepreneurs from venturing into new areas.

How to Develop Women Entrepreneurs?

Right efforts on from all areas are required in the development of women entrepreneurs and their greater participation in the entrepreneurial activities. Following efforts can be taken into account for effective development of women entrepreneurs:

1. Consider women as specific target group for all developmental programmes;
2. Better educational facilities and schemes should be extended to women folk from government part;
3. Adequate training programme on management skills to be provided to women community;
4. Encourage women's participation in decision-making;
5. Vocational training to be extended to women community that enables them to understand the production process and production management;

6. Skill development to be done in women's polytechnics and industrial training institutes. Skills are put to work in training-cum-production workshops;
7. Training on professional competence and leadership skill to be extended to women entrepreneurs. 8. Training and counseling on a large scale of existing women entrepreneurs to remove psychological causes like lack of self-confidence and fear of success;
9. Counselling through the aid of committed NGOs, psychologists, managerial experts and technical personnel should be provided to existing and emerging women entrepreneurs;
10. Continuous monitoring and improvement of training programmes;
11. Activities in which women are trained should focus on their marketability and profitability;
12. Making provision of marketing and sales assistance from government part;
13. To encourage more passive women entrepreneurs the Women Training Program should be organized that teaches them to recognize their psychological needs and express them;
14. State finance corporations and financing institutions should permit by statute to extend purely trade related finance to women entrepreneurs;
15. Women's development corporations have to gain access to open-ended financing;
16. The financial institutions should provide more working capital assistance both for small scale venture and large scale ventures;
17. Making provision of micro credit system and enterprise credit system to the women entrepreneurs at local level;
18. Repeated gender sensitization programs should be held to train financiers to treat women with dignity and respect as persons in their own right;

19. Infrastructure, in the form of industrial plots and sheds, to set up industries is to be provided by state run agencies;
20. Industrial estates could also provide marketing outlets for the display and sale of products made by women;
21. A Women Entrepreneur's Guidance Cell set up to handle the various problems of women entrepreneurs all over the state;
22. District Industries Centers and Single Window Agencies should make use of assisting women in their trade and business guidance;
23. Programmes for encouraging entrepreneurship among women are to be extended at local level;
24. Training in entrepreneurial attitudes should start at the high school level through well-designed courses, which build confidence through behavioral games;
25. More governmental schemes to motivate women entrepreneurs to engage in small scale and large-scale business ventures;
26. Involvement of Non Governmental Organizations in women entrepreneurial training programs and counselling.

Conclusion

Independence brought promise of equality of opportunity in all sphere to the Indian women and laws guaranteeing for their equal rights of participation in political process and equal opportunities and rights in education and employment were enacted. But unfortunately, the government sponsored development activities have benefited only a small section of women. The large majority of them are still unaffected by change and development activities have benefited only a small section of women i.e. the urban middle class women. The large majority of them are still unaffected by change and development. The reasons are well sighted in the discussion part of this article. It is hoped that the suggestions forwarded in the article will help the entrepreneurs in particular and policy-planners in general to look into this problem and develop better schemes, developmental programs and opportunities to the women folk to enter into more entrepreneurial ventures. This article here tries to recollect some of the successful women entrepreneurs like Ekta Kapoor, Creative Director, Balaji Telefilms, Kiran Mazumdar Shaw, CEO, Biocon, Shahnaz Husain and Vimalben M Pawale, Ex President, Sri Mahila Griha Udyog Lijjat Papad (SMGULP).

References

1. Jose P., Ajith Kumar. and Paul T.M., (1994) *Entrepreneurship Development*, Himalaya Publishing.
2. Medha Dubhashi Vinze (1987) *Women Entrepreneurs In India: A Socio-Economic Study of Delhi* - 1975-76, Mittal Publications, New Delhi.
3. Renuka V. (2001) Opportunities and Challenges for Women in Business, *India Together, Online Report*, Civil Society Information Exchange Pvt. Ltd.
4. Starcher, D. C. (1996) *Women Entrepreneurs: Catalysts for Transformation*, Retrieved July 6, 2001.
5. "The Female Poverty Trap" (2001, May 8) *The Economist*, Retrieved March 14, 2001.
6. United Nations Industrial Development Organisation (UNIDO), (1995a) "Women, Industry and Entrepreneurship," *Women in Industry Series*, Vienna, Austria.
7. United Nations Industrial Development Organisation (UNIDO), (1995b), "Women, Industry and Technology," *Women in Industry Series*, Vienna, Austria: Author.
8. Women Entrepreneurs in Poorest Countries Face Formidable Challenges, Including Lack of Training, Credit, Say Speakers at Brussels Forum" [Press Release]. (2001, May 21).

Index

O

P

T

U

V

W

Y